T0234648

# SpringerBriefs in Computer Science

More information about this series at http://www.springer.com/series/10028

Yang-Ming Zhu

# Failure-Modes-Based
# Software Reading

Springer

Yang-Ming Zhu
Solon, OH
USA

ISSN 2191-5768 ISSN 2191-5776 (electronic)
SpringerBriefs in Computer Science
ISBN 978-3-319-65102-6 ISBN 978-3-319-65103-3 (eBook)
https://doi.org/10.1007/978-3-319-65103-3

Library of Congress Control Number: 2017947869

Printed on acid-free paper

This Springer imprint is published by Springer Nature
The registered company is Springer International Publishing AG
The registered company address is: Gewerbestrasse 11, 6330 Cham, Switzerland

*To Alex, Harold, and Xiao-Hong*

# Acknowledgements

I would like to thank an anonymous reviewer whose comments and suggestions helped me improving the presentation of Chap. 1 and the acquisition editor Ralf Gerstner whose comments and suggestions helped me improving the overall flow and examples in various chapters. Last but certainly not the least, I am deeply grateful to my family for their sacrifices of quality family time while I was busy at nights and over weekends writing and revising this book.

# Contents

# Chapter 1
# Introduction

Software has become an indispensable part of our daily life, and our dependence on software is constantly increasing. Software fails, and these failures cost money, time, resources, and sometimes even lives. Software quality is thus critically important.

## 1.1 Software Quality and Quality Assurance

Broadly speaking, software quality has two aspects: functional quality and structural quality. The former refers how well software complies with the functional requirements or specification, while the latter is related to the non-functional requirements and reflects how well software architecture, design, and implementation adhere to standards, principles, and best practices. Poor structural quality does not necessarily cause software issues right away, but it certainly makes software error-prone. Software quality assurance is a systematic approach to improve software quality, and it involves defect prevention, detection and removal, and defect containment activities [57]. We survey some of the most frequently employed techniques below.

### 1.1.1 Software Testing

Software testing is the most frequently used method to detect software defects and improve its quality and reliability. In software testing, a tester runs a software system or its components, executes its functions, observes system behaviors or responses to input, and determines whether the system behaviors conform to its requirements, specification, or expectations. Software testing focuses on its functional quality, and the primary purpose of software testing is to detect defects. Here,

Y.-M. Zhu, *Failure-Modes-Based Software Reading*, SpringerBriefs in Computer Science, https://doi.org/10.1007/978-3-319-65103-3_1

we understand defects intuitively as anything not meeting expectations and defer the discussion of terms such as defects and faults to a later chapter.

Based on the viewpoints a tester takes when designing test cases, testing methods can be classified as black-box testing, white-box testing, and gray-box testing. In black-box testing also known as functional testing, no internal implementation knowledge is assumed and a tester checks the software responses to input and against applicable requirements and specifications. In white-box testing also known as structural testing, knowledge of the software internal working is assumed; test cases can be designed to cover paths through the code, and a tester can compare the actual output with expectations. When only partial knowledge of the internal code structure is assumed, we have a gray-box testing.

Software testing can be performed at different levels or granularities during development, and we have unit testing, integration testing, and system testing. The lowest level testing is unit testing. In different development contexts, the meaning of unit varies. It can be a file or a class. Unit testing typically assumes the white-box testing approach, and it verifies the internal working of the implementation. When multiple units are integrated together, one exercises an integration testing, the purpose of which is to verify that the interface design and interactions among those units are correct. When a complete system is integrated, system testing is performed to verify that the system meets its intended requirements. Development organizations may add additional levels of testing, e.g., subsystem integration testing.

Testing methods can be classified in other dimensions as well. Based on whether a test case is performed manually or automatically, one has automated testing and manual testing. Automated testing is highly desirable for many obvious reasons and becomes the best practice in modern practices. There are still many specialized testings, e.g., smoke testing to check whether there are any basic problems (due to, e.g., an incorrect build). We will not elaborate any further; instead, we refer the readers to books on software testing such as [57] or other taxonomies of testing [21].

Software code can be instrumented, compiled, and then executed or tested, which enables tools to perform runtime error detection. Common defects that can be detected at runtime by dynamic analysis tools include resource leaks, memory leaks, segmentation errors, null pointers, uninitialized memory, and buffer overflow. Runtime error detection tools cannot detect defects which are not in the exercised control path; therefore, it is often augmented or guided with test coverage metrics.

To test software, one needs a running executable, which is not feasible all the time, particularly for software artifacts other than code. The effectiveness of testing depends on test cases, and if there is no test case to exercise a particular path of the code, there is no way to tell whether there is a defect in that path or not. In practice, software testing is supplemented with other quality assurance techniques such as peer review or static analysis.

### 1.1.2 Software Peer Review and Software FMEA

Among all the activities and methods to improve software quality, software peer review or inspection is probably the most effective and commonly performed method besides software testing. Software peer review or inspection started in the 1970s when Fagan published his seminal paper "Design and code inspections to reduce errors in program development" [18], and it has been recognized as the best practice to improve software quality. Software peer review allows peers to detect errors in software artifacts, and the author of the software artifacts can subsequently remove or repair the mistakes and improve the document quality. Empirical evidences accumulated in the past four decades proved again and again that software review is effective (it finds many defects), efficient (it finds defects at a low cost), and practical (it is easy to carry out, and there are standards or procedures to support its application). Software peer review has been applied to all sorts of software projects.

Fagan review has a rigid process, and it is difficult to adopt in globally distributed, rapidly releasing software projects. Chapter 3 discusses various extensions to Fagan inspection. Modern software review, in particular code review, has evolved to a tool-assisted, flexible, lightweight process. Software powerhouses such as Google, Microsoft, and Facebook have all adopted this modern approach, using commercial, open source, or proprietary tools, which allow a developer to submit code changes and invite peers to review, to allow reviewers and author to discuss and annotate code online, and to keep track of issues and their fixes as well as the status of code review activities [53].

At about the same time when software peer review was proposed and practiced, failure mode and effects analysis (FMEA) was applied to software projects as well [51]. FMEA is an inductive, bottom-up method that analyzes the effects of single failure on systems, and Chap. 2 provides an overview of FMEA and software FMEA. Nowadays, software FMEA is applied mostly to safety-critical systems. FMEA allows system designers and implementers to think about the potential problems and figure out how to detect, prevent, or mitigate the problems before they materialize and create a catastrophe; that is FMEA enables engineers to design quality and reliability into a system. Software FMEA is good to exhaustively categorize faults and their effects at a low as well as at a high level, but weak at considering multiple failures. It is widely recognized and documented that software FMEA is tedious and time-consuming to execute, since it involves meetings of subject matter experts and other stakeholders and there are a lot of materials and documentations to go through [42]. Because of this and the fact that there is no established standard to carry out software FMEA, software FMEA has only been applied to safety-critical systems.

### *1.1.3   Other Software Assurance Methods*

There are many other software assurance activities and methods in addition to the above-mentioned testing, software peer review, and software FMEA. In the following, we briefly overview other popular and effective methods and contrast them with software testing, software peer review, or software FMEA when possible.

Fault tree analysis (FTA) is widely used in system reliability and safety analysis. Unlike FMEA, FTA is a top-down, deductive method. It starts with a system-level failure or undesirable event and uses Boolean logic (e.g., AND and OR gates) to construct a diagram known as fault tree to determine what combinations of low-level failures can cause the top-level failure. The partition into low-level causes is done recursively. Improving or removing the low-level failure causes improves the overall system performance. If the nodes in the fault tree are annotated with failure probabilities, one can calculate the failure probabilities for the system or subsystems. FTA was developed in the early 1960s and was applied to software systems in the 1980s. Software FTA is used to find defects during software development and is most effective when detailed requirements or design exists. It is good at analyzing single and multiple failure causes, but weak at identifying all possible failures. Leveson also used it for verifying software code [33]. By combining software FMEA and FTA, Lutz and Woodhouse suggested the bidirectional safety analysis method [38].

Software testing requires an executable and a tester or another program to run it. Thus, it is considered a dynamic method. In contrast to the dynamic analysis, there is a group of methods termed static analysis that does not execute a program. In a sense, software peer review, software FMEA, and software FTA belong to the static analysis category. In fact, the static analysis includes many more techniques; for a partial list, readers are referred to [57]. Nowadays, the static analysis, particularly static code analysis, is almost exclusively reserved for tool-based code analysis. Static code analysis tools exploit various formal methods and heuristics to detect issues with program source code. For example, Astree is based on abstract interpretation of the source code written in C (http://www.astree.ens.fr/). Static code analysis also often checks violation of coding standard or other best practices.

In addition to being used in static code analysis, formal methods such as abstract interpretation and model checking can be used directly to check certain properties of a program or verify program correctness through formal inferences based on mathematical models [57]. As a prerequisite for formal code verification, a formal specification has to be developed. Due to the complexity, associated cost, and lack of expertise, formal methods are typically applied to mission or safety-critical components of a big software system.

In almost all engineering disciplines, models provide necessary abstractions of a physical system so that designers can reason about its properties and correctness. As such, models are often developed before a system is implemented. In software engineering, modeling has a long and rich tradition. The unified modeling language (UML) is extensively used in object-oriented system modeling, analysis, and design. Model-driven development or model-based design has become popular, particularly in embedded control system development [16, 58]. Inevitably, formal methods such as theorem provers and model checking are widely used in model-driven development. There are typically no formal requirements models in model-based design and verification. Instead, a design model is created based on requirements analysis. The design model is used to simulate the system behavior, which provides feedback on the design and requirements. The model-based design enforces continuous testing and verification of the system throughout the design process. In the end, code is generated automatically, which is integrated with possibly other handwritten codes. Static code analysis based on formal methods is applied to verify code for correctness. Model-based design and verification prevents defects and allows early error detection.

Model-based testing is considered an application of model-based development in software testing. Traditionally, test cases are manually crafted and maintained. With model-based testing, test cases are automatically generated from models that describe system behaviors, being it data flow diagrams, control flow diagrams, finite state machines, etc. Typically, test models are manually created from informal requirements and specification models, and thus, model-based testing is considered a lightweight formal method to verify a system. Model-based testing is particularly attractive and effective when it is used with automated testing.

Model-based design and verification, including model-based testing, is becoming popular in the industry, and there are successful case studies in motion control, industrial equipment, aerospace, and automotive applications [9, 16]. It strongly depends on tools or tool chains and their capabilities. However, models are not a good fit for all situations. As an example, recursive data structures are difficult to model. Although we expect the adoption of model-based design is increasing, it is unlikely to penetrate into all industries and application domains.

We have discussed many software quality assurance techniques. Each has its own strength and weakness, and in practice, they are often used in a complementary manner, balancing their cost and benefits [57].

## 1.2 About This Book

This book espouses merits of software peer review and software FMEA and develops a suite of software reading techniques for general software practitioners, including those in organizations that use an agile software development process.

Software peer review is widely regarded as the best practice and most effective method to improve software quality besides testing. Although the formal methods and model-based design are proved to be effective, at least in embedded system development, its wide adoption in software industries and other application domains is yet to happen. We expect that software peer review will remain to be a popular software quality assurance activity for many years to come. It is well established now that defect detection in software review is primarily an individual effort and it happens during individual's preparation. To improve an individual's effectiveness in software review, various reading techniques have been proposed and validated, which direct individuals how and where to find defects in software artifacts. However, it is reported that software peer review often detects trivial issues [41].

Software FMEA is good to exhaustively categorize faults and their effects at a low level as well as high level, particularly when it is compared to software FTA. In fact, identifying failure modes and their effects is critical to software FMEA, and it largely depends on the experiences and skills of analysts or FMEA teams. To make the benefits of software FMEA accessible to general software practitioners, this book develops a series of reading techniques based on common and prioritized failure modes in software requirements, software design, coding, and usability. The combination of software reading and software FMEA essentially focuses the software review on critical and frequently occurring issues in software artifacts while reducing the overhead and tediousness of software FMEA, and it makes the benefits of software FMEA readily accessible to general software practitioners, particularly in small teams and resource-constrained organizations.

The remainder of the book is organized as follows: Chap. 2 overviews FMEA and software FMEA, Chap. 3 overviews the software review procedures and software reading techniques, Chap. 4 presents the basic ideas behind failure-modes-based reading techniques, Chaps. 5–9 discuss the failure-modes-based software reading techniques for software requirements, software design, software coding, software usability, and software testing, and Chap. 10 concludes the whole book.

# Chapter 2
# Software Failure Mode and Effects Analysis

The process of thinking about the potential problems and knowing how to detect, prevent, or mitigate the problems before they create a catastrophe is what failure mode and effects analysis (FMEA) is all about. FMEA enables engineers to design quality and reliability into a system. A variant of FMEA, failure mode, effects, and criticality analysis (FMECA), prioritizes failures and failure modes based on the failure rate and severity of failure effects. Collectively, we use FMEA to encompass both FMEA and FMECA. This chapter provides a general introduction to FMEA and software FMEA.

## 2.1 FMEA

FMEA was first documented as part of the US military procedure MIL-P-1269, titled "Procedures for performing a failure modes, effects and criticality analysis," dated back to 1949. Failures were classified by their impact on mission success and personnel or equipment safety. The later military standards MIL-STD-1269 and MIL-STD-1269A were based on MIL-P-1269.

FMEA was practiced mostly in military and aerospace until late 1970. Ford Motor Company was the first to adopt FMEA in the automotive industry. A broader automotive industry adoption happened in the 1980s, and the joint efforts of a few automotive companies eventually led to the industry standard SAE J1739 published in 1994. The use of FMEA now has been embraced by many industries including aerospace, automotive, nuclear power plant, manufacturing, medical device, and health care.

## 2.1.1  What Is FMEA?

FMEA promotes a systematic way of thinking when a new product or system is developed: what could go wrong, how badly might it be, and how could it be prevented and mitigated. The primary objective of FMEA is to improve design or process. FMEA is a bottom-up, inductive, static analysis method with the effects of failure on lower levels (e.g., individual components) being identified first. FMEA is often performed hierarchically, and the effects identified at the lower level propagate and serve as failure modes at the next higher level [36].

There are many types of FMEA, e.g., system FMEA, mechanical FMEA, electrical FMEA, software FMEA, product FMEA, process FMEA, human-use or misuse FMEA, and health care FMEA. Although the purposes, terminologies, and details vary for each FMEA type, the basic concept is similar.

An FMEA process typically includes the following steps or phases:

(1)  Choose the items to be analyzed,
(2)  Identify the failure modes and root causes for the failure modes,
(3)  Assess the impacts of the failure modes and root causes, and
(4)  Prioritize the failure modes and root causes and identify and implement controls (preventive measures, corrective actions, and compensating provision) to improve the product or process design.

To facilitate the analysis, a spreadsheet is typically used, which can be downloaded from many Web sites or other sources. FMEA is an iterative process, repeated multiple times in the course of product or system development. It is a team effort and often includes meetings of people with different backgrounds and diverse skills and knowledge.

To assess the risk associated with issues identified during an FMEA process and to prioritize corrective actions, some quantitative methods are included. The most commonly used methods for assessing criticality are risk priority number (RPN), criticality number ranking as in MIL-STD-1629A, and multi-criteria Pareto ranking. In the case of RPN, an FMEA team rates the severity of the failure effect, the likelihood of occurrence of the failure cause, and the detection of the failure cause and calculates the RPN as the product of the above three numbers. The rating scales for severity, occurrence, and detection are typically 1 to 5 or 1 to 10. An organization defines a threshold for the RPN value, above which some mitigation is mandatory.

Many authors have written about the benefits of FMEA. FMEA improves product or process reliability and quality and, as a result, increases customer satisfaction. It enables a development organization to identify and eliminate potential failure modes and root causes, which reduces and minimizes late changes and their associated costs. FMEA itself captures an organization's knowledge, catalyzes teamwork, and promotes idea exchanges across teams.

### 2.1.2 FMEA Standards

FMEA has been adopted in a variety of industries, and industry-specific standards have been established. Aerospace and defense companies usually use the MIL-STD-1629A published by the US Department of Defense in 1980. The standard was canceled in 1998, and users instead were referred to various national and international standards. The automotive industry mostly uses the SAE J1739, the first version of which was published in 1994 and the latest in 2009 (the standard for non-automobile applications is SAE ARP5580). Other industries generally adopted the IEC 60812, titled "Analysis techniques for system reliability—procedure for failure mode and effects analysis (FMEA)," published by the International Electrotechnical Commission, and the latest version was issued in 2006. Many professional societies and organizations have published FMEA handbooks or established their own FMEA processes as well, e.g., International Marine Contractors Association Guidance 166 on FMEAs.

## 2.2 Software FMEA

Reifer was widely credited for introducing the FMEA to software engineering for requirements analysis in 1979 [51]. However, there was some precursor work before Reifer, e.g., the software error effects analysis in 1973 [22]. Although software FMEA has been practiced for about 40 years, there is no specific, widely accepted guideline or standard for software FMEA. Researchers and practitioners frequently refer to IEC 60812 for software FMEA. Like hardware FMEA, software FMEA is primarily used to discover the software design issues during software development.

Software is different from hardware. Hardware fails due to aging, wearing, or stressing, but software modules do not fail and just exhibit incorrect behaviors [17]. For software components, the failure modes are generally unknown and depend on the dynamic behavior of the system, since if a failure mode would be known, it would be corrected [17]. The definition of failure modes is one of the hardest parts of software FMEA. Analysts have to apply their own knowledge about the software and postulate relevant failure modes. During software FMEA, possible design failure modes and sources of potential nonconformities must be determined in all software artifacts, mostly codes, under consideration. A complete FMEA for a software-based system should, however, include both hardware FMEA and software FMEA, and the effects should be assessed on the final system functions.

## 2.2.1  Types of Software FMEA

Software FMEA in practice is often performed at different levels, system, sub-systems, and components, which corresponds to architectural partitions or levels of abstraction. The software FMEA file, e.g., a spreadsheet, is treated as a living document, and analysis at different levels can be rolled up. As design and implementation proceed, more details of the system are revealed, which enables meaningful low-level analysis. Goddard suggested the use of software FMEA at a system level and a detailed level on embedded control systems [25], where a system-level software FMEA can be based on the top-level software design and performed early in the software design process and a detailed-level software FMEA can be based on the software module design such as pseudo code and applied late in the design process. Software FMEA at the detailed level can be labor-intensive. Similarly, the committee on the safety of nuclear installations at the Nuclear Energy Agency of the Organization for Economic Cooperation and Development proposed software FMEA at system/division, unit, module, and basic component levels [14].

When conducting software FMEA, analysts take different viewpoints. Bowles and Wan extended Goddard's work and introduced functional, interface, and detailed software FMEA [8], where functional software FMEA is related to functional requirements, interface software FMEA is concerned with the interfaces between software modules and between software and hardware, and detailed software FMEA is conducted on individual variables. The authors suggest to use the results of functional software FMEA to reduce the amount of effort required for the interface and detailed analysis and the results of functional and interface analyses to reduce the effort required for the detailed analysis.

Although researchers and practitioners discussed many different viewpoints, Neufelder's work is most comprehensive and she identified eight viewpoints: functional, interface, detailed, maintenance, usability, serviceability, vulnerability, and software process [42]. The functional viewpoint is mostly useful for software requirements FMEA, the interface viewpoint is for software/software and software/hardware interface FMEA, the detailed viewpoint is applicable to design and implementation FMEA, the maintenance viewpoint is related to software maintenance FMEA, the usability viewpoint is for system use and misuse FMEA, the serviceability and vulnerability viewpoints, as their name suggested, are related to software serviceability and vulnerability, and the software process viewpoint is for software process FMEA.

During software development, many software artifacts are generated. Software FMEA can be tailored to analyze requirements, design, and code implementation. Perhaps the most frequently used areas of software FMEA are requirements analysis and code analysis. In fact, Reifer applied software FMEA to requirements analysis [51]. Code-level FMEA tends to be tedious, and tool assistance is highly desired.

## 2.2.2 Software FMEA Steps

In general, a software FMEA follows the same or similar steps sketched in Sect. 2.1.1. Some authors wrote about an elaborate preparation or planning phase [42], where the hierarchical level (system, subsystems, and components) is decided at which the FMEA is performed, the riskiest parts of the system or subsystem are chosen, as well as the viewpoints to conduct the FMEA are determined. The outcome of an FMEA is documented in a worksheet, and the analysis team needs to pick and agree on the worksheet format. The planning phase can also include team member identification and team formation, resource allocation, software tool customization, documentation (e.g., requirements specification, architecture description, design document, and code modules) identification and preparation, and general agreement on ground rules, assumptions, failure definitions, and policies.

Do not underestimate the effort to prepare information or documentation to support a software FMEA, in fact any FMEA, which may include system architecture or structure, system environment, system boundary, block diagrams, system functional structure (both definition and representation), system initialization/operation/control/maintenance, system and component modeling, failure significance, and compensating provision. This information or documentation defines the extent of analysis and provides the right input to the analysis. It is understandable that, as system design and implementation proceed, they will have different levels of maturity and accuracy.

There is no single widely accepted guideline or standard on the software FMEA procedure. However, there are papers, chapters, and books that discuss software FMEA and its procedures. El-Haik and Shaout elaborated a 12-step software FMEA procedure [17], which is summarized in the following nine steps.

- Define the software FMEA scope. The team lead, along with team members, defines what functions, critical areas, or subsystems and components will be subject to the software FMEA exercise. The team may consult the project scope and architecture description to identify systems, subsystems, or components boundaries.
- Identify potential failure modes. The team can research past failure modes and brainstorm new failure modes with subject matter experts based on new insights on the software under concern. Common failure modes include faulty requirements, interfaces, communications, timing, sequence/order, logic, data, data definition, memory allocation/management, installation, error detection/recovery, false alarm, synchronization, algorithms/computation, user mistakes, user recovery from mistakes, user instructions, abusive user, and incompatibility. While failure modes are identified, related failure causes shall also be identified. Software failure modes are typically caused by design faults or deficiencies, e.g., violation of design principles and best practices. A database or categorization of the failure modes is an important part of corporate knowledge.
- Identify potential failure effects. A potential effect is the consequence of the failure. These effects can be local effects, the effects on the subsystem and

system levels, and the effects on the operator, environment, or other people involved. Fishbone diagrams are often used to capture the cause/effect relationship.

- Rate severity. Severity is a subjective rating and measures how bad or serious the effect of the failure mode is. It is typically rated on a discrete scale of 1 to 5 or 1 to 10, corresponding to negligible to catastrophic effects. Organizations need to provide guidance on how to rate severity, and real examples are highly desirable. Failure effects should be propagated to the system level. The most serious failure modes often need a control plan to mitigate the risks, and the development team needs to develop proactive and preventive design recommendations.

- Rate occurrence. Occurrence is the likelihood that the failure cause occurs in the course of the intended life. It is a subjective rating as well. For software FMEA, it usually assumes that if the failure cause happens, so does the failure mode. Thus, occurrence also measures the likelihood of the failure mode. It is rated on a scale of 1 to 5 or 1 to 10, with highest occurrence corresponding to highest probability and vice versa. The occurrence is just a ranking scale, not the actual probability which would be within 0 and 1 inclusive. Organizations can use historical data to derive the failure rate and use it to guide the assignment of occurrence rating. Researchers also suggested some proxies such as complexity metrics as an indirect measure for occurrence.

- Assess current controls. The purpose of software design controls is to identify, as early as possible, issues such as nonconformities, including not meeting requirements specifications and violating design principles or best practices, deficiencies, or vulnerabilities. To this end, the software FMEA team shall review past similar failure modes and how they were detected, or brainstorm how failure modes can be recognized and detected with new technologies. That is, current controls prevent the cause of failure from occurring. In addition to specific techniques and design verification, design controls also include general design guidelines, best practices, and standards and procedures adopted by the project team such as design review and operator training.

- Rate detection. Detection is also a subjective rating that quantifies the likelihood that a detection method will detect the failure of a potential failure mode before the impact of the effect is materialized. Again, it is a ranking scale of 1 to 5 or 1 to 10, not the actual probability. Common detection methods include review or inspection, assertions, and data validation. The software FMEA team shall assess the capability of each detection method, which may be used in different stages during the development based on their capabilities. The team then reviews all the detection methods, builds a consensus on their detection ratings, and rates the methods. It is important that failure modes with the highest severity are detected directly, close to the failure cause or source, and are compensated immediately and effectively. For failure modes with the lowest severity, they can be detected away from the source, e.g., by the effects of the failure modes; they can be compensated by default values, retry, or other exception handling mechanisms.

- Compute RPN. RPN is simply the product of severity, occurrence, and detection ratings, and it is used to prioritize potential failure modes and root causes. The software FMEA team agrees on a threshold, and when the RPN of a failure mode is above that threshold, the team proposes recommended actions (see next step). There is no universal threshold, since the ratings may be industry or organization specific. The severity, occurrence, and detection, thus RPN, shall be reassessed after a risk mitigation is implemented.
- Recommend actions. Where the risk of a potential failure is high (large RPN), a control plan shall be developed to improve the situation. Potential actions include the following:

  (a) Transfer the risk of failure to other systems,
  (b) Prevent failure altogether, and
  (c) Mitigate the risk of failure by

    – Reducing severity,
    – Reducing occurrence, and/or
    – Increasing the detection capability.

## 2.3  Software FMEA in the Software Development Life Cycle

Various processes or methods are selected for the software development projects, which are known as the software development life cycle models, including the waterfall model, the V model, the iterative model, the spiral model, and the agile model. The V model is nothing but a verification and validation model and often used as a reference model or framework to understand the software development process.

The V model is schematically shown in Fig. 2.1. On the left branch of the V are, from top to bottom, requirements definition, system design, subsystem design, and

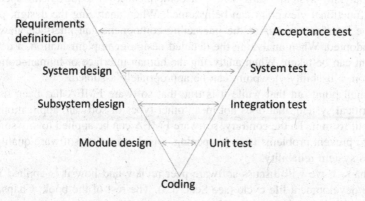

**Fig. 2.1**  The V software development model

module design. On the bottom is implementation or coding. On the right branch of the V are, from bottom to top, unit testing, integration testing, system testing, and acceptance testing, which correspond to the activities on the left branch of V.

The code is often reviewed or inspected to detect anomalies. It can also be analyzed with other static analysis tools. Often the time code or the software unit is unit-tested by execution (dynamic testing). A unit test is to verify that the software unit is implemented per module design. When multiple software modules or components are integrated together, the emphasis is typically on the interfaces among those modules and assumptions one module has on others. System testing is against system requirements specifications and confirms that the system is implemented correctly. The acceptance testing makes sure the right system is implemented from the user's perspective.

Tracing is an important concept in the software development, and the horizontal lines with arrows indicate the tracing between requirements or designs and testing. Every requirements specification and design element shall be tested, and every test shall be traced to system functions. A software system is often implemented using a divide-and-conquer strategy, and the system is decomposed recursively until the lowest element can be adequately dealt with. Thus, there is a tracing on the left side of V from higher-level to lower-level system functions or designs. In line with the hierarchical decomposition, requirements specifications can also be recursively decomposed and refined at system, subsystem, and component levels, which gives rise to system requirements specification, subsystem requirements specification, and component specification, respectively.

Software FMEA can be applied on the left branch of the V, including the implementation at the bottom of the V. The hierarchical levels of software FMEA naturally correspond to the hierarchical decompositions of the system. Software FMEA at a system level can be applied to the requirements definition and system design phases; software FMEA at the subsystem level can be applied to the subsystem design phase; and lastly, software FMEA at the component level can be applied to the module design and implementation phases.

When conducting software FMEA, analysts can take different viewpoints [42]. When analyzing system-, subsystem-, or component-level requirements specifications, a functional viewpoint can be assumed. When analyzing the design, particularly the interface aspects of the interacting components, an interface viewpoint can be adopted. When analyzing the detailed design or implementation, a detailed viewpoint can be taken. When analyzing the human interface or human–computer interaction, a usability viewpoint can be appropriately assumed.

We shall point out that while it is true that software FMEA has been used in safety-critical system, that does not mean other types of software applications will not benefit from it. To the contrary, software FMEA can be applied to any software system to prevent problems from happening, which improves software quality and increases system reliability.

In Chap. 3, we will discuss software peer review and how it is applied in the software development life cycle (see Sect. 3.3). The rest of the book, Chaps. 4–9, discusses failure-modes-based software reading that merges the strengths of software FMEA and peer review and avoids their respective weakness, and illustrates how the failure-modes-based reading techniques can be employed in software requirements (Chap. 5), design (Chap. 6), implementation (Chap. 7), usability (Chap. 8), and testing (Chap. 9).

## 2.4  Summary

This chapter overviewed the history of FMEA, sketched different types of FMEA and main steps in FMEA, and surveyed FMEA standards and guidelines. It then focused on software FMEA. The differences between hardware FMEA and software FMEA were highlighted. The software FMEA steps were illustrated, and how the software FMEA can fit in a software development life cycle was briefly touched upon.

We shall point out that software FMEA is not meant to replace software reliability methods. Rather, software FMEA provides a systematic thinking tool that allows developers to anticipate issues and improve designs. Software FMEA is applicable not just to safety-critical software. All kinds of software projects can benefit from software FMEA.

# Chapter 3
# Software Review and Software Reading

There are many best practices in software engineering, and there is no other practice as prominent as software review or inspection that has enjoyed universal agreement on its effectiveness (it finds many defects), efficiency (it finds defects at a low cost), and practicality (it is easy to carry out). This chapter provides a short introduction to software review or inspection process and software reading techniques that support the software review and inspection.

## 3.1  Software Review and Inspection

Software inspection is a formalized peer review process applicable to any software artifact. It is a static analysis method and was first introduced by Fagan based on his practical experience at IBM in the 1970s [18]. The method was initially intended for design and code inspection and later adapted to inspect virtually any software artifact such as requirements, user documentation, and test plans and test cases as long as such artifacts can be made visible and readable. Fagan inspection has been influential ever since it was published. In fact, the IEEE Standard 1028 is largely based on Fagan inspection [29].

Although software peer review has been practiced for more than four decades, the software literature uses inconsistent and in many cases conflicting terms to refer to the more or less same activities. According to IEEE Std-1028, inspection is "A visual examination of a software product to detect and identify software anomalies, including errors and deviations from standards and specifications" and review is "A process or meeting during which a software product, set of software product, or a software process is presented to project personnel, managers, users, customers, user representatives, auditors or other interested parties for examination, comment or approval." We use the more general term "software review" in this book.

© The Author(s) 2017
Y.-M. Zhu, *Failure-Modes-Based Software Reading*, SpringerBriefs
in Computer Science, https://doi.org/10.1007/978-3-319-65103-3_3

Fagan inspection consists of six steps or operations as originally called: planning, overview, preparation, inspection, rework, and follow-up, as depicted in Fig. 3.1.

We discuss these six steps in the context of design and code inspection. The principal ideas behind Fagan inspection can be applied to inspecting any software artifact.

(1) Planning: The objectives of the planning step are to define inspection entry criteria for the materials subject to inspection, to make the appropriate participants available, and to arrange the meeting place and time.

(2) Overview: The objectives of the overview step are communication and education, as well as assigning the inspection roles to participants. This step involves the whole inspection team. Typically, a meeting is held, during which the project overview and the specifics of the artifact to be inspected are given. The inspection materials are distributed at the end of the meeting.

(3) Preparation: The objective of the preparation step is for the participants to study the material individually to fulfill their respective roles. One of the key ideas in the inspection is to assign different roles to the individual participants based on their respective expertise. The roles of the participants are discussed below. To facilitate the preparation, a checklist of recent error types can be used, or other kinds of reading techniques can be adopted.

**Fig. 3.1** Steps in Fagan inspection

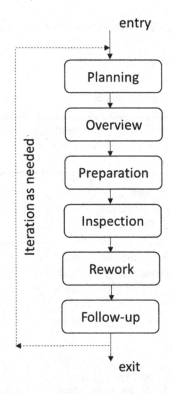

(4) Inspection: The objective of the inspection step is to find errors in the materials under inspection. A formal meeting is held, and the entire team participates in the discussion. At the beginning of the meeting, if code files are under inspection, the implementer (author) can show the implementation of the design. In the course of the meeting, errors are discussed; false positives are dismissed; and true errors are recognized and noted, with possible error type classification and severity identification. It is important to note that the team should not hunt for solution nor discuss alternatives. After the inspection has been held, a written report of the findings has to be released timely.

(5) Rework: The objective of the rework step is to fix all errors or provide other responses. The author of the software artifact is responsible for the rework and responses.

(6) Follow-up: The objective of the follow-up step is to ensure all fixes are effective and there are no newly introduced problems. The moderator decides whether another round of inspection is needed. For example, if the errors are minor and the changes are limited, he can declare there is no need for another round of inspection. Regardless of whether there is another round of inspection, the team needs to pay attention to "bad fixes."

Fagan inspection defines the roles that each participant plays. There are four roles: moderator, author, reader, and tester. The moderator leads the inspection team and takes care of logistics; the other roles represent the viewpoints of those with their respective expertise during the inspection. The moderator is the key person in a successful inspection. He or she possesses strong interpersonal and leadership skills, coaches and guides the inspection team, and handles meeting logistics, including scheduling the meeting and publishing the outcome of the inspection. The moderator must be neutral and objective. The author is the person who created the software artifacts under inspection. The author is responsible for producing the artifacts and fixing errors in the artifacts, with possible help from others. The reader is an experienced peer who can be a subject matter expert on the software artifact under inspection. The tester is responsible for writing and/or executing test cases for the software module or the product.

The Fagan inspection team typically consists of four people, large enough to allow group interaction to detect errors in software artifacts, but small enough to allow individual voices to be heard. To have a healthy group dynamics, an ideal mix of participants can include people with different backgrounds and experience.

Fagan-style reviews have a few noticeable drawbacks. One of them is the heavy process involved, which requires a series of formal meetings and documentations. This limitation is overcome by the introduction of modern lightweight reviews [53]. The other drawback is that the quality of review varies widely, since the participants may be passively engaged with the review. This latter shortcoming is remediated by the active review and reading techniques. Some extensions and improvements to Fagan inspection are discussed in [64].

## 3.2   Software Reading Techniques

Proposed improvements to Fagan inspection often centered on the importance and cost of group meetings, particularly the defect collection meeting (step 4 in Fig. 3.1). There is ample empirical evidence that the software review or inspection is primarily an individual effort and many anomalies are uncovered in the course of individual reading [31, 59]. The individual defect detection performance can vary by a factor of 10 in terms of defects found per unit time, however [26]. To improve an individual's effectiveness, various reading techniques have been proposed and tested. Software professionals were trained to write software documents, but reading, understanding, analyzing, assessing quality, and utilizing the software document are equally important.

### 3.2.1   Software Reading Defined

Software reading is defined as the process by which a developer gains an understanding of the information encoded in a work product sufficient to accomplish a particular task [56]. The term "work product" refers to the software artifact, ranging from requirements specification, design documentation, code files, test plan, test cases, test report, to user documentation. The term "particular task" is related to the purpose of reading, whether the reading is for gaining knowledge of the system, detecting defects, or implementing the design.

Associated with software reading is the software reading technique. A software reading technique is a series of steps for the individual analysis of a textual software product to achieve the understanding needed for a particular task [56]. A series of steps is a set of instructions that guide the reader how to read the artifacts, what areas to focus on, and what problems to look for. It is conceivable that reading techniques can be implemented as guided workflow or instructions in software tools that support software peer review. Software reading is primarily an individual activity.

We read software artifacts to accomplish a particular task. Broadly speaking, we read software for analysis and for construction [2]. In reading for analysis, we read and understand the document and then analyze and assess the qualities and characteristics of the document. The primary objective of reading for analysis is to detect defects in the document. While reading the requirements specifications, we may detect various types of requirement errors such as incorrect facts, omission, ambiguity, and inconsistency. While reading the code, we may detect various types of coding errors such as logic errors, assumption errors, and incorrect function calls. Other objectives of reading for analysis include performance predictions, requirement tracing, and usability. In reading for construction, we attempt to identify whether any requirement, design, code, or test cases can be reused in the same project or in a different project. We also examine the high-level design document to come up with the low-level design, or read the design document to see how we may implement the design properly.

### 3.2.2  Systematic Reading and Unsystematic Reading

There are many reading techniques reported in the literature. Those reading techniques can be classified as systematic reading techniques and unsystematic reading techniques. Ad hoc reading and checklist-based reading fall into the category of unsystematic group (checklist-based reading is sometimes considered as semi-systematic). Perspective-based reading falls into the group of systematic reading, along with many other techniques. These reading techniques collect knowledge about the best reading practices for defect detection into a single procedure. Comprehensive treatment of reading techniques can be found in [64].

The differences between systematic reading and unsystematic reading are best illustrated in Fig. 3.2, where the rectangle shape represents a software artifact to be

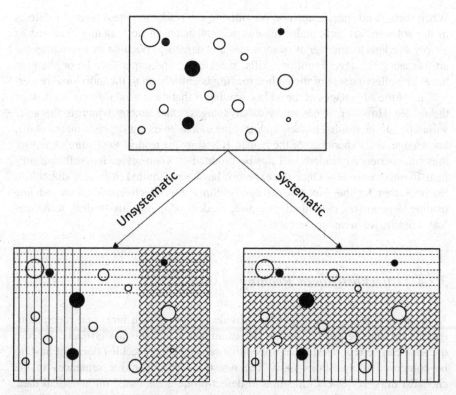

**Fig. 3.2** Comparison of unstructured and structured software reading techniques (adapted from [48])

reviewed, and both open and filled circles of various sizes represent different kinds of defects in the artifact.

To the left of Fig. 3.2 is unsystematic reading, where one or more readers scan through the document and look for defects, which are shaded as vertical, horizontal, or slanted lines. There are at least two problems with that approach owing to its unsystematic nature: (a) There are overlaps on the portions covered by different readers, and (b) there are regions that are not covered by any reader. To the right is systematic reading, where different readers are purposely selected to examine the software artifact, based on their individual expertise. They are also given specific instructions on where and how to detect defects. This ensures that there will be no or minimal overlaps among what they will cover and the entire document is covered. Systematic approaches with specific responsibilities improve coordination and reduce gaps, which increases the overall defect detection effectiveness of the review.

### 3.2.3   Ad Hoc Reading

When there is no specific method provided to the reader to detect issues or defects in the software artifacts under review, we call it an ad hoc reading. The reader simply attempts to uncover as many issues and defects as possible by examining the artifact using whatever intuition, skills, knowledge, and experience he or she may have. The effectiveness of the ad hoc reading is entirely up to the individual reader.

One of the advantages of the ad hoc reading is that there is no training needed for the reader. However, it has many disadvantages, chief among which is the wide variability of the results. In fact, the outcome to a large extent depends on the skills, knowledge, and experience of the reader. It is slow for readers to acquire expertise; thus, inexperienced readers will not be productive when reviewing software artifacts to uncover issues. Once the expertise has been acquired, it is very difficult to teach or transfer the expertise to others. Since the effectiveness of the ad hoc reading depends on individual expertise, readers adopting this reading technique may miss major areas of concern.

### 3.2.4   Checklist-Based Reading

A checklist is a list of questions to provide reviewers with hints and recommendations for finding defects during the examination of software artifacts. Since a question can be rephrased as an imperative sentence, the checklist does not have to be composed of questions only. The questions or imperative sentences in the checklist draw reviewers' attention to defect-prone areas based on historical data. A checklist may also serve other purposes. For example, it can be used to ensure important areas are covered by the artifact under review. Checklist-based reading is semi-structured, as there is no instruction regarding how to use the checklist and how to answer questions in the checklist.

Checklists are typically developed based on the analysis of past team defects in the same or different projects. They can also be based on others' experience, but customized for one's project team. There is a huge collection of checklists in the literature which one can be inspired from [10]. Checklists can be tailored to an individual as well. Individuals can have a personal defect checklist that compiles the problematic areas in which they tend to make mistakes.

Compared with ad hoc reading, checklist-based reading reduces the variability of reading results; i.e., the results are less dependent on the reviewers' skills, knowledge, and experience. It also ensures coverage of important areas and is thus effective at detecting omissions. However, checklist-based reading might detect only the defects of particular types covered by the checklist, i.e., those previously encountered from which the checklist was created. Therefore, insidious defects, which require a deep understanding of the artifacts, are often missed. The other disadvantages of checklist-based reading are related to the checklist itself. The checklist often includes generic items that may not be applicable to the project or the artifact. A lengthy checklist may overwhelm readers.

### 3.2.5  Scenario-Based Reading

Scenario-based reading was developed by Porter and Votta [48], and their paper triggered an active research on software reading techniques. Later on, the method was renamed "defect-based reading" and the term "scenario-based reading" was reserved for a group of reading techniques that use different ways to decompose reading scenarios. Scenario-based reading was motivated by the ideas behind the active design review proposed by Parnas and Weiss [46]. The family of scenario-based reading techniques includes defect-based reading, perspective-based reading, and traceability-based reading. Defect-based reading concentrates on specific defect classes; perspective-based reading focuses on the viewpoints of the consumers of a document; and traceability-based reading traces among requirements specifications and designs and among design artifacts for completeness and consistency.

The scenario used here refers to a process-driven or operational scenario. Scenarios give specific guidance to readers, which can be a set of questions, an assignment, or explicit instructions on how to conduct the review and look for defects. They are expressed in the form of algorithms that readers can apply to traverse the document with a particular emphasis. Because of the detailed guidance, this group of reading techniques is considered systematic. In practice, several scenarios must be combined to provide an adequate coverage of the document, since each scenario is focused, detailed, and specific to a particular viewpoint. To improve effectiveness, the overlap of scenario assignments shall be minimized.

We next discuss the defect-based reading in more detail, since we will compare failure-modes-based reading with it. Readers can refer to [64] for other scenario-based reading techniques.

The main idea behind the defect-based reading is that, if each reader uses different but systematic techniques to search for different, specific classes of defects, he or she and the whole team will have a better chance to detect defects effectively than readers applying ad hoc reading or checklist-based reading. Each reader is given specific steps to discover a particular class of defects, and each reader's role or responsibility is specific and narrowly defined. The defect-based reading technique has been applied to detecting defects in software requirements specifications.

Defect-based reading is based on the analysis of defects in software requirements specification. In general, requirement defects can be divided into two broad types: omission and commission [49]. Depending on what is missing, the omission type can be further divided into missing functionality, missing performance, missing environment, and missing interface. Similarly, the commission type of defects also has four subcategories: ambiguous information, inconsistent information, incorrect or extra functionality, and wrong section.

The above defect taxonomy is used to construct reading scenarios, as illustrated in [49]. For ad hoc reading, the readers are simply given the defect taxonomy. In checklist-based reading, detailed and concrete questions for each defect category, as checklist items, are developed and provided to readers. In defect-based reading, checklist items are substituted with procedures or scenarios designed to implement those checklist items, which lead a reader through the document and give instructions on where and how to find defects. Reading scenarios are developed for different classes of defects and furnished to different readers; therefore, overlapping of efforts is minimized.

## 3.3  Software Reading in the Software Development Life Cycle

During software development, many viewable artifacts ranging from requirements specification, design, code module, to the user interface and test cases, including drawings and diagrams, are generated, which are subject to review or inspection for defect removal. There are many software reading techniques, some of which are general and applicable to many, if not all, software artifacts. We shall use the same V model as in Fig. 2.1 to structure our discussion here as well. In Fig. 3.3, we overlay various reading techniques on top of development phases in the V model. This book presents failure-modes-based reading techniques inspired by software FMEA. Chapter numbers are also given where a particular failure-modes-based reading technique is discussed; e.g., "Code reading, C7" indicates that failure-modes-based code reading is discussed in Chap. 7.

Software requirements specification is a key document generated in the early stages of a software development project. It defines the functionality, scope, and constraints of the software system. It is paramount to read, detect, and correct

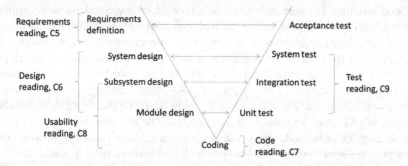

**Fig. 3.3** Software reading techniques applied to various phases in the V software development model

requirements issues early in the development process before they propagate to the downstream activities. It is much cheaper to correct the issues close to where they are introduced. Compared with ad hoc reading and checklist-based reading of software requirements specification, defect-based reading and perspective-based reading are proved to be more effective. This book discusses failure-modes-based requirements reading in Chap. 5.

The development of software architecture and design lies between requirements engineering and code implementation. Thus, software design needs to satisfy a requirements specification and provide guidance to subsequent implementation. For software design reading, a reasonable assumption is that the requirements specification as input is free of error. The focus of design reading is to make sure the design is correct and complete with respect to requirements and the design itself is consistent and clear and has adequate information to start the subsequent detailed design and implementation. Design reading is crucial since the design quality directly affects the quality of and effort required for the implementation. In addition to the general reading techniques such as ad hoc, checklist-based, and perspective-based reading, specific design reading techniques include usage-based reading and traceability-based reading [64]. Usage-based reading employs prioritized use cases to focus readers' attention on what matters most to end users. Traceability-based reading is applicable to inspecting object-oriented (OO) designs. The family of traceability-based reading includes seven techniques organized as horizontal reading and vertical reading, with the semantic checking as a theme across both. Horizontal reading ensures all design artifacts are consistent among themselves, and vertical reading ensures designs are consistent with the requirements specification. Which reading technique to use depends on the availability of design diagrams and descriptions. It certainly requires coordination between all readers using different reading techniques on different artifacts. This book discusses failure-modes-based design (including architecture design and software interface design) reading in Chap. 6.

Code modules are perhaps the most reviewed or inspected software artifact. General reading techniques such as ad hoc, checklist-based, and perspective-based reading have been applied to code reading. There are specific reading techniques for code, however [64]. Stepwise abstraction is a classic technique and was developed mostly for procedural programming. As the OO programming paradigm gained popularity, the intrinsic complexity of OO code reading became evident. Abstraction-driven reading technique is meant to deal with the strong delocalization inherent to OO code. To cope with the unpredictable dynamic behavior of an OO system from its static code view, use-case-driven reading can be used as a complement. This book discusses failure-modes-based code reading in Chap. 7.

Usability is typically related to user interfaces and how a user interacts with a system. Usability issues can be uncovered through usability reading instead of usability testing. Heuristic evaluation, cognitive walk-through, and guidelines and checklists are common analytical techniques in practice. Perspective-based usability reading is also reported [64]. Usability reading can be conducted against user interface mock-ups in design or fully prototyped or implemented user interfaces, and thus, usability reading can happen in both design and implementation phases. This book discusses failure-modes-based usability reading in Chap. 8.

Testing-related artifacts such as test cases and report shall be reviewed as well. Ad hoc reading and checklist-based reading can be employed. Perspective-based reading can provide a tester's perspective; however, it has not been used to read test artifacts directly. Test reading can happen in unit testing, integration testing, or system testing phase. Acceptance testing sometimes happens on the user's organization, and the development organization may not be involved. Thus, the development organization may not be involved in acceptance test reading. This book discusses FMEA-based test reading in Chap. 9.

Like design patterns [23], software reading techniques codify best practices for software review and inspection. It is expected that those techniques will be tailored to your unique circumstances for their best effectiveness. You could customize, modify, subset, or extend a reading technique, or combine good ideas from multiple reading techniques to create your own.

## 3.4  Summary

Software review or inspection is the best practice in software development with a long history. Software professionals are trained to write software documents, but reading, understanding, analyzing, assessing quality, and utilizing the software document are equally important. To improve an individual's effectiveness in software review, software reading techniques are developed. This chapter reviewed the software inspection procedures and focused on common software reading techniques such as ad hoc, checklist-based, and scenario-based reading. The role of software reading was also emphasized in the software development life cycle. According to a recent industry survey [13], ad hoc reading is used in 35% of the software reviews, and checklist-based reading is used in 50%. About 10% of the reviews use some specific or advanced reading techniques such as scenario-based reading, and the remaining 5% use simulation or other techniques. The rest of the book focuses on a new family of software reading techniques based on failure modes and their root causes.

# Chapter 4
# Failure-Modes-Based Software Reading

Before discussing failure-modes-based software reading, this chapter first lists definitions of common FMEA terms. It then surveys software failure modes and root causes that tend to be common to a class of software. With that preparation, this chapter introduces the main ideas of failure-modes-based software reading and the motivation for it. How the failure-modes-based reading is applied to requirements, design, code, usability, and testing is elaborated in later chapters.

## 4.1 FMEA-Related Terminologies

Researchers and practitioners use FMEA-related terms inconsistently, oftentimes contradicting with each other. Even the same person may use the same terms in different contexts but mean different things, or use different terms to refer to the same concept. We do not intend to define or standardize terms here. Rather, we list reasonable definitions and meanings in the literature so that readers are aware of them and decode their meanings from contexts.

IEEE Standard "Classification for Software Anomalies" uses the term "anomaly" to refer to any abnormality, irregularity, inconsistency, or variance from expectation [30]. An anomaly can be a condition or an event, an appearance or a behavior, and a form or a function. The standard defines failure, defect, fault, error, problem, as well as their relationship.

According to the IEEE Standard, a **failure** happens when a system or a system component does not perform a required function or it performs a required function but not within specified limits. A failure is an event related to termination or loss of function. A **problem** is simply the consequence of a failure, including difficulty, uncertainty, or negative situation that is experienced by a person when interacting with the system.

A failure is caused by a **fault**, which is the manifestation of an error in software (e.g., an incorrect step, process, or data definition), and characterized by an inability

© The Author(s) 2017
Y.-M. Zhu, *Failure-Modes-Based Software Reading*, SpringerBriefs
in Computer Science, https://doi.org/10.1007/978-3-319-65103-3_4

to perform a required function. Fault is a state, as distinguished from failure which is an event. A fault is inserted or injected into the software by a human **error**, which is an action that produces an incorrect result.

A fault is a subset of **defect**, which is an imperfection or deficiency in the software that does not meet requirements or specifications. Defects need to be repaired or replaced. The IEEE Standard makes a clear distinction between a defect and a fault. Every fault is a defect, but not every defect is a fault. A fault is related to the system's dynamic behavior and encountered during software execution. A defect is not a fault if the defect is detected by inspection or other static analyses and removed prior to software execution.

When conducting a failure analysis or a root cause analysis, analysts typically trace a failure to program fault, where the offending culprit programming code is identified. From the offending program code, they trace to human errors, development process issues, and tool deficiencies. Pareto analysis can be followed to identify significant errors, issues, or deficiencies, so that a targeted improvement can be implemented.

Irrespective of IEEE Standard and other standards, the loose usage of faults, defects, and failures among software engineering researchers and practitioners is still pervasive, even in a narrowly defined context such as code review. Mantyla and Lassenius cited three different viewpoints of the term "defect" in the code review literature, from narrower to wider breadth: defects as failures, defects as faults, and defects as deviations from quality [41].

**Failure mode** is often defined as the way in which a failure occurs or is observed. **Failure effect** is then the consequence(s) a failure mode has on the operation, function, or status of an item. There are local effects, component- or subsystem-level effects, system effects, environment effects, and operator or human effects. For example, failure of a medical device may have a negative effect on patients being diagnosed or treated or on operators operating the device.

The definition of failure mode is based on hardware FMEA. As discussed in Sect. 2.2, software is different from hardware and software does not fail due to aging, wearing, or stressing; rather, software modules just exhibit incorrect behaviors. Failure implies that the system or component was once able to perform its function, which is true for hardware. For software, if it does not perform the required function under a specific circumstance, it was not able to do so from the very beginning of the operation. That is, software does not break and the ability to perform a function is never terminated or lost. Software does not fail. Thus, some researchers and practitioners prefer fault modes and treat FMEA as Fault Mode and Effects Analysis [52], where **fault mode** is defined as one of the possible states of a faulty item for a given required function. For the purpose of this book, we will not make a fine distinction and just call them failure modes.

## 4.2   Catalogs of Software Failure Modes

What software failure modes an analyst can identify during software FMEA depends on his or her expertise and familiarity with the software under analysis. Many potential failure modes are common to a class of software, and the corresponding preventive and corrective actions are also common [1]. As an organization typically works on one specific kind of software, the team has probably accumulated some experience on the failure modes, e.g., based on past defects and field reports. Other sources to study failure modes include papers, books, and standards. In this section, we survey failure modes and root causes.

As we will go through the failure modes reported in the literature, one may find different ways to define failure modes, which are called functional failure modes and structural failure modes [14]:

- Functional failure modes are concerned with the effect on system functions under consideration, e.g., failure to provide a response to user actions.
- Structural failure modes also include failure causes. For example, "frozen sensor" not only describes the failure consequence on the functionality, but also provides the reason for failure.

For software components, design and implementation flaws are typical causes of failure; thus, design and development process shall be considered in software FMEA. Additional causes may include software requirements errors, user misuse, unexpected external events, or deployment environment.

Researchers and practitioners have published numerous software failure modes in the past. There is no complete set of failure modes, although a comprehensive set of failure modes is highly desired to ensure no critical conditions are missed and all critical conditions are analyzed during software FMEA. Researchers and practitioners generally agree that it is unlikely that anyone can identify a complete set of failure modes, which depends on the nature and complexity of the system [52].

A survey of the literature returns the following:

- Reifer compiled a list of major failure modes based on the analysis of three software projects. These failure modes include computational, logic, data I/O, data handling, interface, data definition, database, and others [51].
- Becker and Flick described failure modes for their application which include hardware or software stop, hardware or software crash, hardware or software hang, slow response, start-up failure, faulty message, checkpoint file failure, internal capacity exceeded, and loss of service [5].
- Lutz and Woodhouse analyzed failure modes along the dimensions of data and processing of data [38]. Any system or any functional part of a system can be abstracted as the logic structure of input-processing-output (IPO). In case of data (input to and output of a component), potential failure modes include missing data, incorrect data, timing of data, and extra data. For data processing, potential failure modes include halt or abnormal termination, omitted event, incorrect logic, and incorrect timing or order.

- Ristord and Esmenjaud listed general-purpose failure modes at a processing unit level: The operating system stops, the program stops with a clear message or without a clear message, and the program runs, producing obviously wrong results or apparently correct but in fact wrong results [54].
- Wallace and Kuhn analyzed 15 years of recall data and summarized failure modes (primary symptoms of failure as they called) in medical device software [61]. Their list includes the following 13 items: behavior, data, display, function, general, input, output, quality, response, service, system, timing, and user instruction.
- Neufelder categorized failure modes into faulty functionality, faulty timing, faulty sequence, faulty data, faulty error detection and recovery, false alarm, incompatibility, faulty network communication, faulty synchronization, faulty logic, faulty algorithm or computation, faulty memory management, misuse, abuse, and faulty installation [42]. Clearly, she implicitly treated failure modes as fault modes. Additionally, she identified many root causes for each failure mode and mapped failure modes to different viewpoints for software FMEA.
- The research information letter [52] reviewed the literature and came up with 11 sets of system-level functional failure modes on digital instrumentation and control systems from different sources. The authors synthesized a set of failure modes as a superset, which includes the following:

  1. No output upon demand. The system failed to provide (updated) output upon demand and for any input,
  2. Output without demand,
  3. Output value incorrect,
  4. Output at incorrect time,
  5. Output duration too short or too long,
  6. Output intermittent,
  7. Output flutters, i.e., unwanted oscillation or fluctuation,
  8. Interference that affects another system, and
  9. Byzantine behavior, which is an arbitrary behavior in a distributed system as a result of failure or fault.

  The authors make a clear distinction between failure modes and fault modes. The number of software faults and fault modes is much large, and the authors did not try to synthesize them.

Standards often provide examples of failure modes. There is no standard for software FMEA, and failure modes in standards are generally concerned with hardware. However, some of them are appropriate to software as well. IEC 60812 gives tables of examples of typical failure modes [28]. "Failure mode/mechanism distributions, 2016" contains over 990,000 records of failure modes and mechanisms (i.e., causes) on parts and assemblies from the databases at the Reliability Information Analysis Center [19]. The Chinese standard, GJB299C-2006, lists 442 failure modes and their frequencies [24]. In addition to the public databases and records, many organizations maintain their own private databases to support FMEA.

Software FMEA based on failure modes databases or libraries was recently reported [11, 27]. Huang et al. used the same IPO logic structures to classify failure modes, and they classified failure modes as input failure, process failure, and output failure. Considering the importance of time-sequencing, they divided each category into two subcategories, data failure and time-sequence failure. There are 43 failure modes in their general failure modes database. For example, there are eight general failure modes in the data input failure mode subcategory and four general failure modes in the time-sequence input failure mode. In addition to the general failure modes database, there is a specific failure modes database, which captures the concrete failure modes. Corresponding to specific means of input, there are specific failure modes associated with keyboard input, file input, etc. One hundred and eighty-four specific failure modes are captured in the specific failure modes database. Chen et al. took a step further [11]. They ontologically annotated failure modes in the database and provided a search and retrieval capability based on semantic similarity, which facilitates the reuse of failure modes during FMEA.

## 4.3   Failure-Modes-Based Reading

We espouse merits of software reading and software FMEA and develop a failure-modes-based software reading. Software review augmented with failure-modes-based reading focuses reviewers' attention on critical issues. The tedious, laborious, time-consuming, and error-prone nature of software FMEA is alleviated, and the essence of software FMEA is made accessible to general software practitioners. By no means, we intend to replace software FMEA, particularly for safety-critical systems.

### 4.3.1   Comparison of Software Review and Software FMEA

Since its introduction, software review has been practiced for almost 40 years in almost every industry. Software FMEA was introduced around the same time, and so far, it is mostly used in safety-critical systems. The primary reason for its limited adoption is probably that software FMEA is tedious, laborious, time-consuming, and error-prone to carry out, particularly for the code-level, detailed analysis.

Although software review and software FMEA are both meant to improve software quality, there are some differences. Software review or inspection looks for typical software problems, while software FMEA is a tool for anticipating failure mode effects and eliminating them whenever possible. For software review, software artifacts subject to review must be available and viewable. For software FMEA, however, nothing prevents the analysis team from brainstorming failure modes and effects, root causes, and mitigations, as long as the input and output of the system are known. There are even claims that software FMEA is more effective than traditional software review or inspection [42]:

- Software review and inspection often focuses on style instead of failure modes,
- Software review and inspection often identifies (local) issues instead of system-wide effects of issues, and
- Software review and inspection often does not target high-risk areas.

## 4.3.2  Ideas Behind Failure-Modes-Based Software Reading

Software components and systems can fail in different ways, and the ways in which they fail to perform as intended or according to specifications can be categorized as failure modes. In fact, one of the important activities in software FMEA is to identify failure modes. The values organizations derive from software FMEA largely depend on the quality of failure modes identification.

For each failure mode, there can be one or more root causes. While failure modes postulate what could be wrong, root causes underpin why it is wrong. The ideas behind failure-modes-based software reading are to use failure modes and their root causes to guide the software reading process. Failure modes tell the reader what to look for, root causes provide guidelines where to look, and the reading technique provides steps to read and detect defects in the software artifacts. If these defects are left behind, the software could fail as failure modes suggest.

Defect detection in failure-modes-based reading is guided by priority which is simply the effects of failure modes and root causes at the system level, provided the effect prioritization is available. Organization can build a risk knowledge-base with respect to severity, occurrence, and detection of failure modes and root causes and use them to set priority.

Failure-modes-based software reading is schematically illustrated in Fig. 4.1. "Software artifacts to review" and "Supporting or related documents" are the input, but only the former is subject to review and defect detection. The output is a list of issues. Artifacts to be reviewed can range from requirements specifications, design diagrams and descriptions to code modules and related documents, user interface mock-ups, test plan, etc. Supporting and related documents can be anything that is helpful. If there is an FMEA worksheet filled in already, it can be used. Even a general list of failure modes, root causes, and effects can be helpful as well. For architectural reading, the system requirements specification can help readers understand the system and architectural drivers. For code reading, design diagrams and interface specifications generated in the design phase can be provided so that readers can trace design to implementation.

Assume failure modes $FM_j$ (j = 1, 2, ..., J) have been identified, and for each failure mode $FM_j$, there are $RC_{jk}$ (k = 1, 2, ..., $K_j$) potential root causes. The list of failure modes and list of root causes can be sorted by their priorities in decreasing

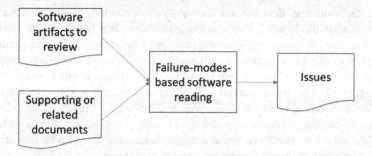

**Fig. 4.1** Input and output for failure-modes-based software reading

A. Read and understand the software artifact X and related documents.
B. For each failure mode $FM_j$ (j=1, 2, ..., J)
    a. For each root cause $RC_{jk}$ (k=1, 2, ..., $K_j$) leading to $FM_j$
        i. If root cause $RC_{jk}$ exists in or related to the artifact X, but is not mitigated satisfactorily, log an issue.
        ii. If root cause $RC_{jk}$ does not exist in or is not related to the artifact X and is beyond the system control or scope (i.e., it is an external failure cause), and there is no mitigation or the failure and risk of failure are not mitigated satisfactorily, log an issue.

**Fig. 4.2** Instructions for failure-modes-based software reading

order. Failure-modes-based software reading has steps as shown in Fig. 4.2, where no time limit on reading is assumed.

When failure-modes-based reading is applied in practice, the reading can be time-boxed or rank-based. In time-boxed reading, one allocates a fixed amount of time and divides the allocated time to failure modes proportionally by their priority weights. Therefore, critical failure modes are allotted more time and examined thoroughly. In rank-based reading, however, the failure modes are examined in the order of their priority and there is no preset time limit except the whole allocated time for reading. For each of the reading schemes, the reading procedures can be easily modified to suit the constraints.

## 4.3.3 Why Failure-Modes-Based Reading?

Software FMEA is a very expensive undertaking, since it involves a cross-functional team of many participants in a series of meetings [42]. Additional limitations and disadvantages include the following: It is often a manual and tedious process, the outcome depends on the analyst's knowledge and accuracy and completeness of the input documentation, and a complete list of failure modes is hard to come by. Alternatively, software reviews or inspections are often conducted in practice to detect and correct software issues. Modern software review is light-weighted, informal, asynchronous without meeting, and often supported by specialized tools [7]. An important supporting technique for software review or inspection is reading technique [64]. Ad hoc reading, checklist-based reading, defect-based reading, and perspective-based reading have been reported with success in industry use. However, those reading techniques do not take into account lessons learned on software failure modes and root causes.

Here, we combine the essence of software FMEA with software review or inspection and create a failure-modes-based software reading technique. This reading technique is meant for individual use during software review and analysis. It guides reviewers during software review, focuses them on potential failure modes and root causes of the failure modes, and enables them to identify and mitigate incorrect, incomplete, and missing critical features. Compared with software FMEA, the reading technique is light-weighted without series of big meetings. Compared with existing software review and supporting reading techniques, the new reading technique explicitly draws readers' attention to potential failure modes, root causes, and mitigation. Failure-modes-based software reading is intended to take advantages of both software review and software FMEA. It can be used during individual preparation work as part of software FMEA; it can also be used for individual reading as part of software review or inspection.

Compared with software review and reading techniques, particularly defect-based reading, failure-modes-based reading uses failure modes and their priorities, rather than defect classification, to direct the reading focus. It is risk-driven. Most importantly, it directs readers to check whether failure root causes are removed and failure modes are mitigated. Defect-based reading, however, does not provide any support on defect root causes and mitigation mechanisms. Failure-modes-based reading is applicable to requirements, design, code, usability, and test plan, as will be discussed in later chapters. Defect-based reading has only been applied to requirements specifications.

Software FMEA is a team effort, and it requires strong commitment. Organization may not have formal software FMEA in place, and a small organization or development team may not have the required resources. Failure-modes-based reading makes the benefits of software FMEA readily accessible.

We shall point out that, in software review, it is generally agreed that defect collection meeting is not necessary or at least practitioners do not emphasize it anymore. In fact, the whole industry is converging to a tool-assisted, meeting-less review. At the time of this writing, the meeting is considered an important and critical part of FMEA, since brainstorming and discussion are an integral part of the method.

## 4.4  Summary

This chapter listed common terms used in software FMEA to facilitate a shared understanding and surveyed the literature on recurring failure modes and root causes. Failure modes, root causes, and their mitigations tend to be common to a class of software. Although it is impossible to define a complete set of failure modes for all kinds of software, it is important and feasible to compile a comprehensive list of failure modes for a particular kind of software to ensure all critical conditions are considered and analyzed in practice. This chapter then introduced failure-modes-based software reading, which combines merits of software review and software FMEA. This reading technique draws readers' attention to critical issues with software, while avoiding the typical overhead associated with software FMEA. Failure-modes-based reading makes the benefits of software FMEA readily accessible to general software practitioners, particularly in small teams and resource-constrained organizations.

# Chapter 5
# Failure-Modes-Based Requirements Reading

This chapter discusses the importance of software requirements in the software life cycle. It then surveys the common failure modes and root causes in software requirements and presents the failure-modes-based requirements reading technique.

## 5.1  Introduction

FMEA was introduced to software engineering by Reifer in 1979 [51]. In fact, software FMEA was first proposed to be applied to requirements analysis. Since then, the idea has been validated and extended by many authors [25, 34, 38, 42, 62]. For example, Lutz analyzed the root causes of software requirements errors in safety-critical, embedded systems such as spacecraft [34] and came up with a safety checklist for use during requirements analysis [35]. She and her colleagues combined software FMEA (forward search) and fault tree analysis (backward search) to identify ambiguous, inconsistent, and missing software requirements in critical spacecraft software [37, 38]. Failure modes were analyzed using two tables, data table and events table, in accordance with the message passing model of distributed systems. The data table was used to analyze the communication failures, and the events table was used to analyze the process failures.

It was not unexpected that FMEA was applied first in requirements analysis, given the importance of a software requirements specification (SRS) in software development life cycle. An SRS is generated in the early stage of a software development project. It defines the functionality, scope, and constraints of a software system. A good SRS shall be a SMART one: specific, measurable, attainable, realistic, and traceable [40]. The importance of the SRS cannot be overemphasized enough. If the development is based on an incomplete and incorrect SRS, the finished software product will not fulfill users' needs. Defects in a vague or ambiguous SRS can be propagated down to subsequent development phases. At best, designers or developers will catch these problems, but at the expense of

© The Author(s) 2017
Y.-M. Zhu, *Failure-Modes-Based Software Reading*, SpringerBriefs
in Computer Science, https://doi.org/10.1007/978-3-319-65103-3_5

potential schedule delay and cost overrun. At worst, the defects remain undetected and a faulty software product is delivered to users, which could cause damage to users' environment. It is thus paramount to detect and correct requirements issues early in the development process.

Defects such as incorrect, incomplete, or missing requirements in SRS can be caught in SRS review. They can also be caught using software FMEA conducted from different viewpoints. The most relevant viewpoint for requirements analysis is, however, the functional viewpoint [42].

## 5.2  Requirements Failure Modes and Root Causes

Software can fail in different ways. Identifying and classifying failure modes and root causes is of practical significance. Section 4.2 provides an overview of failure modes. The literature also includes specific failure modes for software requirements. A short summary of failure modes and root causes relevant to software requirements is in order.

Porter, Votta, and Basili classified defects in software requirements specifications into two types, omission and commission, which are the bases for their defect-based reading of SRS [49]. Based on the discussion of terminology in Chap. 4, defects here are faults or root causes of software failures. For an omission-type defect, important information is missing from an SRS and it can be further divided into four groups: missing functionality, missing performance, missing environment, and missing interface. For a commission-type defect, incorrect, redundant, ambiguous, or conflicting information is captured in an SRS and it has four subcategories as well: ambiguous information, inconsistent information, incorrect or extra functionality, and wrong section.

There are other defect taxonomies. IEEE Std 1028-2008 categorizes anomaly (defects) as missing, extra (superfluous), ambiguous, inconsistent, not conforming to standards, risk-prone, incorrect, unachievable, and editorial [29], which is more or less in agreement with that of Porter et al.

Lutz reported that safety-related software errors tend to have different causes than non-safety-related errors and errors in identifying, understanding, and communicating functional and interface SRS often contribute to safety-related errors [34]. Functional faults include operating faults (omission or unnecessary operations), conditional faults (erroneous condition or limit values), and behavior faults (incorrect behavior, not conforming to requirements). Interface faults are understood in a broad sense and refer to any interactions with other system components such as data, control transfer, or timing, regardless if the interface is defined explicitly or implicitly. She also proposed a safety checklist [35], specifically to improve the SRS in the mentioned areas.

In a recent literature survey, Walia and Carver took a step further by attributing faults or defects to their sources, including people errors, process errors, and documentation errors [60]. Under people errors are errors of communication, participation, domain knowledge, specific application knowledge, process execution, and other cognition; under process errors are errors of inadequate method of achieving objectives, management, elicitation, analysis, and traceability; and under documentation errors are errors of organization, no usage of standard, and specification. Although linking software failures to program faults, human errors, and process flaws was studied extensively [34], Walia and Carver's work was comprehensive and considered the body of knowledge of psychology, human cognition, and human error.

Neufelder categorized the common failure modes in SRS as follows: faulty functionality, faulty timing, faulty sequencing or state transition, faulty data, and faulty error handling [42]. We further discuss those failure modes below, taking into consideration other researchers' works mentioned above.

**Faulty functionality**. Almost all SRSs are prone to this faulty functionality failure mode. Requirements typically specify what the system should do in normal operations, but often fail to state what the system should not do in the case of abnormal events (negative requirements) and how to detect and recover from those events. An SRS often contains hidden or unstated assumption, which is well understood among people who are familiar with the software being specified. Negative requirements are one common type of unstated assumptions. As use case is frequently used to capture requirements, misuse cases are proposed to capture negative requirements [20].

In a defensive requirements specification, one should include worst-case scenarios [35]: how the software shall respond to extreme conditions, extreme values, or boundary cases, hardware failure or malfunctioning, unexpected states, out-of-ordered events, invalid or stalled data, data overflow or buffer overrun, etc. To guard against those cases, runtime data checking, validation, and assertion can be added as requirements.

SRS is developed or compiled one item by one item, sometimes by different requirements engineers. For a large system, it is possible to have conflicting SRS. Thus, common causes for a faulty functionality failure mode include incomplete SRS, SRS with unstated assumption, conflicting SRS (with other SRSs or with itself), and SRS with extraneous information.

**Faulty interface**. Interface shall be part of SRS, be it the interfaces between hardware and software, or one software component and another software component. Interfaces are a major source of safety-related software errors [34, 35]. Interface is related to the final system partitioning which is considered part of system design. Here, one should focus on the interfaces between those software and system components known at the specification time. Requirements faulty interface is concerned with incorrect interactions between software components and other system components, which can be caused by missing (missing interface specification) or incorrect (incorrectly specified interface) system inputs to the software components and software component outputs to the system, as well as timing dependencies (real time, interrupt handling, etc.), hardware capabilities and limitations (buffering, noise characteristics), communication links, and operating environments.

**Faulty timing**. In general, a faulty timing failure mode is applicable when an SRS is related to events or communications, but it can happen to any SRS. Consider if required operations happen too soon or too late, or if a timer interval is too big or too small. This is often considered as performance failure mode [62], and performance SRS can be either missing or incorrectly specified. When the arrival of events on the system is beyond the system processing capacity, the system behavior shall be specified whether events can be dropped.

A race condition can occur when multiple execution units try to access the same data or hardware, but the access is not serialized or synchronized. While the performance failure mode may not generate wrong answer, race conditions typically create incorrect answers or undesirable behavior.

**Faulty sequencing or state transition**. This is applicable when an SRS is related to events or state transitions. A faulty sequence failure mode can happen when an SRS describes the order of operations incorrectly. If the system has multiple constituent components or subsystems, the start-up and shutdown sequence can be important due to interdependencies.

When the system can be represented as a finite state machine, a faulty sequence failure mode can also happen when there is a missing state transition or incorrect state transition in a group of SRSs, or there is a dead (not the end state) or orphan state (not the start state). An orphan state is unreachable, and a dead state cannot be transitioned to other states.

**Faulty data**. Faulty data failure mode is applicable when a SRS is related to data. All software systems manipulate data, one way or the other. Data can become faulty when a SRS results in an incorrect data or output, or the data in a wrong format or wrong unit of measurement, or the timing of the data is either too late or too early, or when the accuracy of the data is inappropriate (either too tight or too loose). Input or output data can have four postulated faults: absent data, incorrect data, wrong timing of data, and duplicate data [38].

**Faulty error handling**. Most SRSs are prone to this failure mode, e.g., missing error handling. Error handling, also known as exception handling or fault management, can be at fault or missing. Root causes for faulty error handling failure mode could be related to state, data, timing, or sequencing. A faulty error handling happens when a SRS fails to specify how to detect a failure, report the failure, recover from the failure, or contain the failure. Some practitioners advocate a fault management specification which includes requirements on reliability, and availability, in addition to fault management. False positive also falls into this category. For any required operations, consider the consequence if the system is unable to perform, unable to perform correctly, or able to perform but generates a bad result.

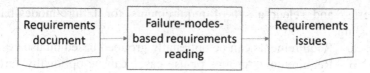

**Fig. 5.1** Input and output of failure-modes-based requirements reading

## 5.3   Failure-Modes-Based Requirements Reading Techniques

A failure-modes-based requirements reading technique is depicted in Fig. 5.1, where the input is the requirements documents and output is a list of requirements issues. It is assumed that requirements readers have a basic knowledge of common requirements failure modes and root causes, which is not listed as input explicitly.

Based on the requirements failure modes and root causes discussed above, we have the following failure-modes-based requirements reading instructions (Fig. 5.2).

The reading instructions are based on discussions of failure modes, root causes, and their mitigation in Sect. 5.2. For a failed step, a reader can optionally perform an error abstraction (what caused the errors in requirements specification) and check whether the same error causes produced other incorrect SRS.

## 5.4   Example

Traffic lights are familiar to many people, and this universal symbol is frequently used as an analogy. For an imaginary system, the requirements engineer determined that it is important to monitor the system's health as part of the fault management, and the system uses the traffic lights such as green, yellow, and red to signal system's health. Part of the SRS is shown below (adapted from [42]), and there is no other related SRS on the same aspect of the system:

- SRS-01: The system shall display a green light if there are no detected system and component failures and no detected system and component warnings.
- SRS-02: The system shall display a yellow light if there are no detected system and component failures and at least one detected system and component warning.
- SRS-03: The system shall display a red light if there is at least one detected system and component failure.

Overall, the SRS includes some fault management specifications and each SRS item is uniquely labeled in this example, which are all good. It is not clear, however, what shall be the initial or default state of the traffic light. This is not critical as

A. Define and select a set of requirements for failure-modes-based reading.
   a. Requirements can be optionally grouped based on use cases.
   b. Requirements groups or use cases can be optionally further prioritized based on importance to users and criticality to system safety or mission.
B. For each requirement, or for each requirement in a requirements group, in sequential order or priority order if applicable
   a. Verify that the requirement is unambiguous and SMART (specific, measureable, attainable, realistic, and traceable), or satisfying other well-formed requirements criteria.
   b. Verify that the requirement is documented in the right section and belongs to the right requirement group.
   c. Identify related requirement items if not already available.
   d. Locate a list of failure modes and root causes in requirements your organization may have; if the list does not exist, continue with e.
      i. For each failure mode and root cause applicable to the requirement under examination, search how the failure mode and root cause is handled. If there is no specific handling and the effects of the failure mode are critical, log an observation against the requirements with details. In the end, go to step D.
   e. Focus on faulty functionality failure modes.
      i. Verify that there are no inconsistent or conflicting, and redundant requirements. A requirement can conflict with itself or other requirements.
      ii. If a negative requirement is needed, verify that the negative requirement exists, and there are details on how the negative events are detected and recovered from.
      iii. Verify that there are no hidden, unstated assumption behind the requirement.
      iv. If worst-case scenarios requirements shall be included, search and verify their existence.
      v. Based on your understanding of the application domain, verify that there is no requirement with extraneous information, there is no missing functionality or environment, and there is no

**Fig. 5.2** Instructions for failure-modes-based requirements reading

incorrect or extra functionality.

f.  Focus on faulty interface failure modes.

    i.  Refer to the system block diagram(s) and identify major system components and interactions between them. Identify requirements on hardware/software and software/software interfaces.

    ii.  Verify that there is no missing interface specification.

    iii.  Check system inputs to software components and software component outputs to the system, timing dependencies, operating environments, etc. Verify that all interfaces are correctly specified.

    iv.  For software/hardware interface, verify that the assumption on the initial hardware state is correct.

g.  Focus on faulty timing failure modes.

    i.  If timing aspect is important (if required operations happen too soon or too late, or if a timer interval is too big or too small), verify that the performance requirement exists and is correctly specified.

    ii.  Verify that the system behavior is specified when the event arrival rate is beyond system capability.

    iii.  When multiple, independent software components read and write the same data, verify that the system state is well defined.

h.  Focus on faulty sequencing or state transition failure modes.

    i.  If the requirement is not related to events or state transitions, skip this.

    ii.  If the requirement describes an sequence of operations, verify that the order of these operations is correct.

    iii.  If there are multiple components or subsystems which are interdependent, verify that the start-up and shut-down sequences are correct.

    iv.  If the system is represented as a finite state machine, draw the state transition diagram and verify that there is no missing state transition, all state transitions are correct and allowed, and there is no dead state or orphan state.

i.  Focus on faulty data failure modes.

    i.  Identify the data input and output.

**Fig. 5.2**  (continued)

      ii.  Verify that the data unit of measurement is correct.

    iii.  Verify that the data accuracy is appropriate.

    iv.  Verify that the data format is specified and correct.

     v.  Verify that timing of data is neither too late nor too early.

j.   Focus on faulty error handling failure modes.

      i.  For a critical requirement, verify that there are specific steps to detect/report a failure, and recover from the failure or contain the failure when the system is unable to perform, unable to perform correctly or timely, or able to perform but generates a bad result.

C.  If any steps in (B) fail, log an issue with specifics as well as suggestion for improvement if possible.

D.  Sort the list of issues logged above based on the severity of impacts and likelihood to happen so that they can be prioritized for a targeted improvement.

**Fig. 5.2** (continued)

long as the system status is correctly monitored and the traffic light is updated accordingly. For example, if the initial state is green, but there is a warning or error in some components, the traffic light will be updated to yellow or red. On the other hand, if the initial state is red, but there is neither warning nor error in the system or components, (we hope) the traffic light will be updated to green. Current SRS does not cover this behavior, however (see below discussion). It can also be the case that the monitor actively pulls the system and component status at start-up and then sets the initial light accordingly. The desired behavior is not specified; thus, this is a functionality failure.

It is not clear whether the monitoring component continuously pools the status of each component or the components notify the monitor their status. How they interact shall be part of the interface specification, which is missing (an interface failure).

There are timing-related failures as well. If the monitor pulls the component status, it is not clear how often it shall pull them. If the components notify the monitor their status change, it is not clear how soon the components shall notify the monitor once they detect a status change. It is not specified either how soon the system or component failures shall be detected once they occurred. Additionally, it is not specified how soon the traffic light shall be updated once the monitor knows a status change.

We now turn to the state transitions. The traffic light is modeled as a finite state machine, and we have the following transition table, where the leftmost column indicates a begin state and top row shows an end state. The state transition table is filled in based on the given SRS:

|        | Green                     | Yellow                    | Red      |
|--------|---------------------------|---------------------------|----------|
| Green  | No failures;<br>No warnings | No failures;<br>Warnings | Failures |
| Yellow |                           | No failures;<br>Warnings  | Failures |
| Red    |                           |                           | Failures |

Although implied, there are no defined state transitions from yellow to green, from red to green, and from red to yellow. Once the light became red, there is no clearly defined condition to change its color. Once the light became yellow, it can only change to red, but not back to green. They are dead states. There are missing specifications how to detect and clear the warnings and failures: Shall it be done automatically, or shall it involve human intervention with, for example rebooting?

We could also consider the case that when different components are hosted on different computers, how they can communicate and update the status reliably, what are the requirements specifications for delayed or lost status update, etc.

## 5.5 Summary

This chapter applied failure-modes-based software reading to software requirements specifications. A software requirements specification defines system functionality, scope, and constraints, and it is important to get it right to avoid expensive rework in downstream project phases. This chapter surveyed requirements-specific failure modes and root causes, based on which the specific requirements reading instructions were devised. A contrived example was discussed to illustrate how the reading techniques can be used in practice.

# Chapter 6
# Failure-Modes-Based Design Reading

Software design plays an increasingly important role in software development, particularly as the scale and complexity of software increase. In this chapter, we focus on architecture design and interface design, survey failure modes and root causes at each level of design, and discuss failure-modes-based reading of architecture and interface.

## 6.1 Introduction

Software works, not by itself or by accident. Designers have to purposely craft it [4]. If software design was neglected or a design mistake was made at the early stage of development, it will take longer to correct. One may still remember the crashes of the US health insurance marketplaces Web site, healthcare.gov, when it initially launched in early October 2013. After the Patient Protection and Affordable Care Action became a law, the health insurance marketplaces were set up to facilitate the purchase of health insurance in each state. Due to design flaws, perhaps caused by incompatible components from different contractors, and an unanticipated surge of traffic, the Web site crashed when customers signed up and applied for coverage. The problems were fixed not until early December 2013, with many people working around the clock and at a price tag estimated to be $121 million.

Software architecture plays a pivotal role not only during development and deployment phases, but also in later maintenance. It is reported that maintenance, including adding new functionalities, fixing defects, and modifying the software to improve its quality, can cost as much as 90% of the total cost of a typical software project [32]. Any improvement to software architecture design that helps developers to easily understand source code will improve the project cost. The tensions between traditional software architecture and agile methods are well recognized; however, the importance of architecture is being acknowledged, particularly for

© The Author(s) 2017
Y.-M. Zhu, *Failure-Modes-Based Software Reading*, SpringerBriefs
in Computer Science, https://doi.org/10.1007/978-3-319-65103-3_6

large software systems built using agile methods, and practitioners started to build an architecture runway in the early stage of an agile project.

Failure modes in software architecture design include two aspects: (1) whether the design meets the requirements and (2) whether the design can make future maintenance easy. Failure modes in the first category have to be fixed or mitigated; otherwise, the system will not meet its intended use. Common design errors include not meeting significant requirements, extreme conditions neglected, forgotten cases or steps, and loop control errors [55].

The second aspect is related to bad design practices where common design practices and principles are violated. Although they are unlikely to cause failures directly, they may do it indirectly, since in general they make a software system difficult to understand, maintain, and evolve and thus are error-prone. The relationship between bad designs and software quality might be based on personal experiences or anecdotes without much scientific data to support. D'Ambros and colleagues recently reported that design flaws do correlate with software defects after the software applications are deployed to the field and an increase in the number of design flaws in software is likely to yield more defects [15].

## 6.2  Architectural Design Reading

Architectural design is concerned how to partition a system into various components and use those components to satisfy system requirements. Interaction of those components is through defined interfaces, which are discussed in the next section. When architects and designers design the system, they typically follow working solutions from the past, which are codified as architecture styles and design patterns, taking into account design principles and balancing different, sometimes conflicting quality requirements [23].

A software architecture serves many critical roles, including as a communication vehicle among stakeholders and a blueprint for software development. We can have user-level and developer-level architectures. Use-case diagrams are considered user-level architecture. They model user needs, capture the proposed system functionalities, are typical outcomes of requirements modeling and analysis, and serve as a communication vehicle to users. Use-case description is part of system requirements. Developer-level architectures include class diagrams, state diagrams, sequence diagrams, and interaction diagrams, and their audience is developers. Activity diagrams and sequence diagrams are frequently used to show how use cases are realized. We here focus mostly on the developer-level architecture.

## 6.2.1  *Architectural Design Failure Modes and Root Causes*

The objective of software design is to fulfill software system requirements using architectural elements, their interactions, as well as properties and configurations of both. For safety-critical systems, the design has to ensure safe operation, i.e., under any failure conditions, the system must be in a safe, deterministic state. Key fault management aspects have to be identified and incorporated into the software architecture, which addresses fault detection, isolation, recovery, and reporting. Goddard proposed a system-level software FMEA that is performed early in the design process to assess the fitness of software architecture, i.e., whether the top-level functional partition of the system can provide protection from the effects of potential software and hardware failures [25].

A typical fault management architecture shall have the following elements: fault detector, fault monitor, and fault handler [6]. At the lowest level is the fault detector, which detects a malfunction in hardware and software components. A fault monitor monitors multiple or all fault detectors and relays their status to a fault handler, and the latter determines which components failed and takes an appropriate action. If the system has a hierarchical design, there may be additional components to aggregate and then forward status information to upper-level elements.

Software design can fail to address critical requirements, including the fault management elements mentioned above. This is a typical omission type of error. It can also be the case that the requirements are only partially addressed.

A software system can fail if it is exposed to unexpected operating environments. Thus, the software shall be designed to cope with different or changing deployment environments. The system can fail in the presence of transient or permanent hardware failures. If the system is expected to have a high availability, an uninterruptible power supply (UPS) can be used against the power outrage. The network connection can be disconnected occasionally, and the software shall detect it and retry to connect. Data nowadays is acquired and streamed to cloud for storage and processing. If continuous processing of the acquired data is expected, the system can provide a local, on-premise processing capability in case it is disconnected from the Internet, probably with degraded performance.

In addition to the unexpected physical environment, a software system can fail when it receives incorrect input from other interoperating systems or humans. At runtime, a system can fail to perform tasks due to resource conflicts or limitation. For microcontroller or device driver software, it can fail due to incorrect interrupt, blocked interrupt, incorrect interrupt return, or failed to return, etc. For safety-critical systems, the design shall have defined safe states in the presence of failures.

Each system function can be abstracted as input–processing–output blocks on design level and failure modes can present in each block. Data failure modes in the input block and output block are similar and include data in unsafe range, wrong hardware interface, wrong data type, delayed input or output, early input or output, and frozen data.

In the processing block, to prevent failures and failures propagation, inputs shall be validated and the output shall be checked as well. The processing results shall be checked whether software has executed correct functions in the right order. Processing failure modes include wrong decision, computation, loop, logic, task failure handling, task scheduling. The processing itself can fail to execute, execute incompletely, generate incorrect result and at incorrect timing (too early, too late, or slow).

To improve computational performance and thus throughput, concurrency is often exploited in design. Concurrency is typically represented in design as branches or forks in activity diagrams. However, concurrency is prone to failure. Each individual task needs to be correct, and multiple tasks have to be coordinated to avoid race conditions, deadlocks, and load imbalance.

A design can fail to constrain how a design shall be implemented. Different programming languages support different features, and some features can be error-prone. Designers can limit the usage of certain programming constructs. To develop safety-critical systems, development tools and libraries shall be validated, and designers can specify validated development tools to use and third-party libraries to include. Unsupported features or compiler-specific behaviors are certainly discouraged.

A good architectural design meets requirements, anticipates, and addresses issues during development and after deployment. Most software systems have a long lifetime and will be actively maintained and extended. To make software easy to understand, maintain, and evolve, designers often follow best practices and apply design principles such as separation of concerns, single responsibility principle, principle of least knowledge, do not repeat yourself, keep it simple. Best practices and key principles now are packaged as architecture styles, design patterns, and coding idioms. In practice, however, design best practices and key principles are not followed consistently. Instead, designers frequently adopt some bad practices, which researchers and practitioners call anti-patterns, design smells, or code smells. Code smells will be discussed in the next chapter.

Contrast to design patterns which codify proven and reusable solutions to commonly occurring design problems within a given context, an anti-pattern is a recurring solution to a design problem that generates negative consequence. Anti-patterns are bad solutions. Unlike design patterns to show designers what to do, anti-patterns teach designers what not to do. God class or blob is probably the most frequently mentioned anti-pattern, which knows about or controls too many other classes, has many different responsibilities, and has complicated dependencies. Some symptoms of a god class include too many methods and attributes. Similar to god class, a brain method is a very large method that contains many conditional branches, deep nesting levels, and many variables. Criteria for god class or brain method may sound subjective; software metrics can be used to quantify dependency, complexity, depth of inheritance, coupling between objects, etc.

Although design patterns are good practice in general, they can be misused or applied incorrectly. Singleton is probably one of the first a few design patterns designers learned. However, it can be misused or abused, and excessive use of singletons is called singletonitis. Some inexperienced designers tend to bend all design problems to the patterns they know. They treat design patterns as a golden hammer, and every design problem looks like a nail.

Design smells refer to structures that are violations of design practices and principles and lead to negative design quality. An anti-pattern may have one or more design smells, and commonly occurring design smells become anti-patterns.

### 6.2.2 Failure-Modes-Based Architecture Reading Techniques

The failure-modes-based architectural design reading is schematically shown in Fig. 6.1, where the input to the reading is architecture diagrams and description such as activity diagrams and sequence diagrams, and a software requirements specification. The software requirements specification is assumed to be correct, used to guide the reading, and thus not subject to review for defect detection. The output of the reading is a list of architectural design issues.

The architectural design reading can start when the design team has developed an initial architecture and has allocated or mapped functional requirements to the architectural elements. Readers can examine the design to detect potential deficiencies and assess whether the software architecture meets the requirements, provides protection from the effects of hardware and software failures, and facilitates future software evolution.

Based on the above discussion of software architecture failure modes and root causes, we present the failure-modes-based software architectural design reading instructions in Fig. 6.2.

Step A simply identifies safety and mission critical requirements. Step B then traces them to architectural design to see whether the architecture fails to address them or address them partially, and whether the mitigations are in place to deal with potential failure modes and root causes. Step C checks whether the architecture description has properly constrained an implementation. Step D assesses the overall

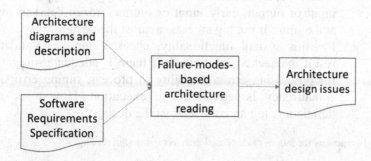

**Fig. 6.1** Input and output for failure-modes-based architectural design reading

A. Read the requirements specification and identify critical (safety, mission, etc) functionalities if not already identified.

B. For each of the identified critical functionalities in A, trace it to the architectural design.

    a. If you cannot trace it to architectural elements, log an issue against the design.

    b. If you can trace it to architectural elements, examine the design to verify that the design adequately meets the requirement; if not, log an issue against the design.

    c. Locate a list of failure modes and root causes in architectural designs your organization may have; if the list does not exist, continue with d.

        i. For each failure mode and root cause applicable to the design under examination, search how the failure mode and root cause is handled. If there is no specific handling and the effects of the failure mode are critical, log an observation against the design with details. In the end, go to step C.

    d. If the system will be exposed to adverse environments (e.g., transient or permanent hardware failures, loss of power, loss of network connection, receiving incorrect data, constrained system resources to perform tasks, incorrect interrupt, blocked interrupt, incorrect interrupt return, or failed to return), evaluate if the design is still sound, search for any mitigation, and assess the sufficiency of mitigation. Log an issue against the design if you see any flaws.

    e. If it is a safety-critical function, search for safe states in the presence of any failures; if no such states defined, log an issue against the design.

    f. For this system functionality, check if there is any mechanism designed to deal with data failure modes (unsafe range, wrong hardware interface, wrong data type, delayed input or output, early input or output, frozen data) in input and output; if no, log an issue against the design.

    g. For this system functionality, check if input is validated, result is checked; also check if there is adequate mitigation for processing errors, inability to process, timing errors, or concurrency issues related to execution. If you see any deficiency, log an issue against the design.

**Fig. 6.2** Instructions for failure-modes-based architectural design reading

C. If an implementation of the design shall be constrained (language, prohibited features of language, validated tools, proven middleware/libraries, compiler settings, build process, etc), search for it in the design document. If you cannot find it, log an issue. If you find it, but feel it is not adequate, log an issue. Conversely, if improper constraints exist, make an observation as well.

D. Read and understand the overall design and all design elements. If you see general design principles and practices are violated (anti-patterns, improperly applied design patterns, or design smells), make an observation.

E. Sort the list of issues logged above based on the severity of impacts and likelihood to happen so that they can be prioritized for a targeted improvement.

**Fig. 6.2**  (continued)

maintainability of the architecture by evaluating it against common design principles and practices. The list of best practices and key principles can be defined and expanded by the organization as needed.

## 6.3  Interface Reading

Large software systems are often partitioned into subsystems or modules which are assigned to different teams or organizations for design and implementation. In the end, those subsystems and modules are integrated and assembled through defined interfaces. Interface design is an important part of architectural design. Flawed interface design can induce system-wide bad consequence on performance, reliability, or robustness, prolong system integration, and cause expensive last-minute design and implementation changes. We single the interface design out due to its prominent roles in software architecture and development.

A well-defined interface separates concerns, decouples interacting parties, reduces interdependencies, allows each evolution independently, and enables software reuse. An interface is a shared boundary across which two components exchange information, either data or commands. The interface can be between software and hardware or between software and software. Humans also exchange information with machines, mostly through user interfaces, which will be discussed in a later chapter on usability. In the case of software/software interface, it can be between two internal software modules, between software module and database or other services, between internal and external software modules, etc.

We shall not limit to the application programmer interface (API)-like interfaces. In some programming languages, there is an interface type or an abstract class that can be used to define an interface. In addition to the explicitly defined interfaces, interface can assume other different forms. Ozarin listed serial bus message, shared memory, queue message, API, memory-mapped hardware interface, and interrupt and interrupt service routines as commonly used interfaces [43, 44].

### 6.3.1  Interface Failure Modes and Root Causes

Interface failure modes can be systematically explored using the interface viewpoint during software FMEA [42]. Causes of software interface problems can in general be attributed to either (1) defective interface definition or (2) unexpected operational performance [44]. Missing specification of a measurement unit or a valid parameter range is an example of defective interface definition; delay in data reception or corrupted data is an example of unexpected operational performance. We discuss common interface failure modes and root causes below [42, 44].

Interface can fail due to faulty definition failure mode, which includes missing, incomplete, ambiguous, or inappropriate interface design. Compared to a requirements specification or architectural block diagram, an interface definition between two modules can be completely missing. This can be troublesome when different assumptions on the interface are made during development and the inconsistency is only discovered at a later integration.

Data is frequently passed through interfaces. The interface definition is incomplete if the units of measurement (if applicable) for the data items are not specified. If the values are relative, measurement zero points shall also be included. For example, length can be in units of meters, centimeters, or inches, and time can be stated in different time zones. If the interface is meant for one party to provide data and the other party to consume, the frequency of data update shall also be specified, as well as the tolerance of the frequency deviation and expected behavior if the data is not provided and consumed at the specified rate. When binary data is passed across different system, the data representation, e.g., little endian or big endian, shall be defined. The valid range of parameters shall also be included. Additionally, make it clear who, caller or callee, is responsible to check the data validity.

Interface definition typically has a natural language description, which can include the precondition and postcondition of the interface call, and in what context the interface shall be used. The description can be ambiguous due to the imprecision of natural languages. Variable names in the interface definition shall be chosen with care. Meaningful names or established names in the technique domain shall be used.

Inappropriate interfaces can have many forms. The interface can fail to meet the requirements or architectural design. The interface, although meeting requirements and design, can fail to deliver system performance (see chatty interface below). The interface specification requires specific technology that can increase system's overall cost without proper justification.

Interface can fail due to unexpected operation performance or environment. When software components communicate across machine boundary via a network, the communication failure mode due to the loss of network communication or the network congestion shall be considered and coped with.

At runtime, one component sends processing commands to another component. The processing failure mode can occur due to incorrect command, no command, or resource limitation. To send or process a command, system resources are consumed. It can happen that the system has not enough resource to send or process command, or too many commands are sent or received to overwhelm the system.

Software systems typically integrate third-party solutions such as commercial off-the-shelf (COTS) components. When using third-party solutions, the interface versioning is critical, in addition to the above-mentioned processing failure modes and root cause. Mismatching interfaces cause at least compilation failure. Even worse, the semantic of the interface can change, which causes hard-to-track runtime failure. Software applications may depend on middleware, such as enterprise service bus or Java virtual machine, or operating systems such as Windows or Linux. As technologies evolve, certain interfaces or system calls may become deprecated or obsolete, particularly in the early phase of the technology development. Database is employed in many systems. The database migration must be planned to handle large amount of data and data in different format. As Internet of Things and data analytics become pervasive and popular, database interfaces and components shall be prepared for the upcoming needs and associated failures.

Interface can fail on time-related aspects known as timing failure mode. How often two interacting components exchange data sometimes is critical. If it happens too often, many data are exchanged, which may pump too much data to the network and tie up system resources. If two components exchange many small amounts of data across network, the system may suffer performance issue, since each small message has an overhead. Chatty interfaces shall thus be avoided in a distributed environment. On the other hand, if it happens less often, components may have stale data. When multiple components coordinate to accomplish a task, those components shall be synchronized and work shall be balanced to improve throughput and avoid starvation. If multiple components share data, data access, particularly data update, shall be guarded to avoid race condition.

System dynamic behaviors are often modeled with collaboration or sequence diagram. Components send messages in particular order to fulfill a specific system functionality. The order of the interface calls can be wrong, and the associated failure mode is called sequencing failure mode.

When two components send and receive messages through the defined interfaces, data is passed along, which can go wrong in different ways (data failure mode), including missing or incomplete data, corrupted data, incorrect data, incorrect data format (type, size, unit). When two components continue to send and receive data, the data may duplicate, come late, or come out of order. This might not be a problem in strongly typed systems, but certainly poses a challenge in weakly typed software, e.g., the data is encoded in an XML stream or a binary object.

While the faulty error handling in the requirements focuses on error handling related to requirements, faulty interface error handling focuses on error handling in communications between different components of the system, particularly between software and hardware devices. Specifically, faulty interface error handling can occur when device errors are falsely detected or detected incorrectly, device errors are not detected, there is a wrong or no recovery from device errors, or communication channel with the device becomes unavailable, etc.

### 6.3.2  Failure-Modes-Based Interface Reading Techniques

In a software system, there can be many interfaces. Failure-modes-based interface reading focuses on failure modes associated with software/hardware and software/software interfaces and provides reading instructions to uncover potential issues. For maximum benefits, one can choose interfaces deliberately for reading. Good candidates include complex interfaces that are error-prone, core interfaces that support critical system functions, and interfaces that are designed by inexperienced teams.

For a given interface, one shall first identify which software component provides the interface and which software components consume the interface. One shall pay attention to not only what the software shall do, but also what the software shall not do.

The failure-modes-based interface reading technique is schematically shown in Fig. 6.3. The input to the failure-modes-based interface reading includes the interface design and its description, the requirements specification, and architecture block diagrams. The interface design and description is subject to review, and the other input documents provide necessary background for readers to understand the interfaces, the needs of interfaces, and their contexts. The interface design may be in the form of UML diagrams or other graphical formats, but we do not dictate its representation. The output of the interface reading is a list of interface issues. The issues shall be sorted based on their perceived effects judged by the readers.

Based on the common interface design failure modes and root causes, the failure-modes-based interface reading instructions are given in Fig. 6.4.

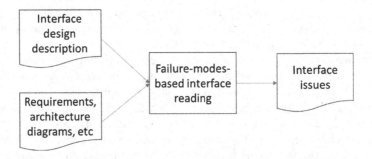

**Fig. 6.3** Input and output for failure-modes-based interface reading

A. Understand the system and critical interfaces.
  a. Read the requirements specification and architectural block diagrams if available, identify the critical (safety, mission, etc) parts of the systems if not already identified, and identify interfaces related to those critical parts.
  b. For each of the identified critical interfaces, identify who provides the interface, who consumes the interface, what parameters are involved and their characteristics, and what is the expected behavior of the interface call.
B. For each of the identified critical interfaces in A, verify its design and description is present in the interface design document; otherwise list the interface as missing.
C. For each of the critical interfaces documented in the interface design document, examine it in details.
  a. Locate a list of failure modes and root causes in interface designs your organization may have; if not, continue with b.
    i. For each failure mode and root cause applicable to the interface under examination, search how the failure mode and root cause is handled. If there is no specific handling and the effects of the failure mode are critical, log an observation against the interface design with details.
  b. Check completeness of the interface. Log an issue against the interface if any of the following is true: missing data items that should be part of the interface, missing the type of a data item, missing the valid value range of a data item, missing units (if applicable) of a data item, missing measurement zero points (if applicable) of a data item, missing rates and range for data update, missing behavior specification if data is not updated in the acceptable rate, missing data format specification, etc.
  c. Check unambiguity of the interface. Log an issue against the interface if the description lacks clarity, the semantics of the interface is not clearly documented, the name of the interface as well as the names of the data items causes confusion, etc.
  d. Check appropriateness of the interface. Log an issue against the interface if any of the following is true: the interface cannot fulfill its intended purpose; if implemented, the interface will degrade the system performance or other

**Fig. 6.4** Instructions for failure-modes-based interface reading

quality attributes; the interface is hard or unjustifiably expensive to implement; data items that should not be included listed; etc.

e.  Check communication failure modes. Log an issue against the interface if the interface is meant to be used by components across machine boundaries, but there is no handling of communication loss and network congestion.

f.  Check resource failure modes. Log an issue against the interface if the interface processing consumes system resources, but the interface design does not consider resource limitation.

g.  Check COTS failure modes. If the interface depends on third party software, log an issue if any of the following is true: interface versioning and compatibility are not considered; the third party interface is misused; deprecated or obsolete third party interface is used;

h.  Check timing failure modes. Log an issue against the interface if any of the following is true: the frequency at which two parties exchange data through the interface is inappropriate; there is no handling if the data exchange rate is deviated from the specification; it is a chatty interface; race condition can happen, but is not dealt with; load imbalancing can happen, but is not dealt with; etc.

i.  Check data failure modes. Log an issue against the interface if any of the following is true: data passed through the interface can be missing, incomplete, corrupted, in wrong format, etc, but is not dealt with; lost data, duplicated data, delayed data, out-of-order data, etc. can happen, but is not considered;

j.  Check error handling failure modes. Log an issue against the interface if any of the following is true, particularly for software/hardware interface: device errors are falsely detected or detected incorrectly; device errors are not detected; there is a wrong or no recovery from device errors; communication channel with the device becomes unavailable, etc.

k.  Check relationship among interfaces. Log an issue if any of the following is true: multiple interfaces shall be called in particular order, but not specified; data can be passed to a

**Fig. 6.4**  (continued)

module through two different interfaces concurrently, but out-of-order data arrival or delayed data receiving is not dealt with; data can be sent to different interfaces for redundancy, but false-positive and false-negative error checking is not handled.

D. Sort the list of interface issues logged above based on the severity of impacts and likelihood of happening so that they can be prioritized for a targeted improvement.

**Fig. 6.4**  (continued)

## 6.4  Example

Body mass index (BMI) is frequently used to assess how much an individual's weight deviates from what is normal for his or her height. Although BMI has different variations and its normal range depends on age, gender, and race, it is in wide use for preliminary diagnosis due to its simplicity (https://en.wikipedia.org/wiki/Body_mass_index).

Suppose an interface is defined to allow client software to calculate BMI, given mass (weight) and height:

```
float ComputeBodyMassIndex(float mass, float height);
```

What issues do we see with this simple interface design?

Mass represents one's weight. However, the unit of mass is not specified: Shall it be pounds, kilograms, or some other units? Similarly, the unit of height is not specified: Shall it be meters, centimeters, feet, or inches? Without specifying units, the interface is not complete and hard to guarantee it will be used as intended. To fix this, the interface description shall include the proper units.

Weight and height are all positive numbers. It is not clear how the function will respond when negative or zero values are passed in. Should an exception be thrown or should a default value be returned to signal a problem encountered? If a default value is returned, what is that default value, zero, a negative number, or some other number? Even when positive mass and height values are passed, it is not clear whether proper range checking is performed or not. For example, more than 500 or less than 1 kg as mass, or more than 3 or less than 0.2 meters as height is unlikely to encounter in real life. To remediate that, the behavior of the interface shall be documented.

BMI is typically defined as body mass (in kilograms) divided by the squared body height (in meters) according to Adolphe Quetelet. However, other definitions are possible, and height scaling powers other than 2 were suggested as well. As part of the interface definition, a formula indicating how the BMI shall be calculated communicates unambiguously among designers, implementers, and clients.

For the simple calculation like BMI, timing performance and resource usage are not critical and we will not elaborate further.

## 6.5   Summary

Software architecture plays an increasingly important role in modern software development. In safety and mission critical applications, it has to ensure safe system operation under any failure conditions. This chapter focused on architecture and interface designs of a software system, surveyed failure modes and root causes in those designs, and presented reading techniques for them, making use of the common failure modes and root causes. The objectives are to detect, remove, and mitigate common failures and adversary impacts.

# Chapter 7
# Failure-Modes-Based Code Reading

Software source code is the most frequently read software artifact, and it is advocated that software FMEA shall be conducted at the code level to be most effective. This chapter discusses the most common code failure modes and their root causes and presents a failure-modes-based code reading that uses the common code failure modes to direct code reading activities.

## 7.1 Introduction

Software FMEA is frequently conducted at the code level, and some practitioners argue that software FMEA is best performed at the code level to make the code more robust. Software FMEA at the code level is to determine whether any single software variable with unintended values assigned can cause specific catastrophic events or other serious effects. Since variable values are assigned as a result of some sort of calculation, algorithm failure modes are also the focus of software FMEA. Code-level software FMEA is intrinsically tedious and error-prone; thus, tools are being researched and developed to automate the process [45, 50].

Neufelder suggested to adopt the detailed, maintenance, or vulnerability viewpoints when conducting the code-level FMEA [42]. In this chapter, we are concerned with the most common code failure modes related to both functionality and maintainability. There are code failure modes for specific applications such as database or Web, which are not covered here. We will not discuss security vulnerability issues, either. Common Weakness Enumeration compiled top 25 most dangerous software errors since 2009, and the most recent third iteration was released in 2011, which can be used for code reading to detect the vulnerability.

Coding errors have been studied and classified by many researchers. For example, Basili and Selby classified coding defects as initialization, data, interface, control, computation, and cosmetic [3]. The orthogonal defect classification of IBM is influential in the industry [12]. The most comprehensive one perhaps is due to

© The Author(s) 2017
Y.-M. Zhu, *Failure-Modes-Based Software Reading*, SpringerBriefs
in Computer Science, https://doi.org/10.1007/978-3-319-65103-3_7

Mantyla and Lassenius [41], who synthesized the research before 2009 and classified defects as functional and evolvability ones. The discussion in this chapter is primarily based on their work.


## 7.2   Code Functionality Failure Modes and Root Causes

Functional defects affect software runtime behavior and may cause system failure when code containing the defects is executed. Based on their technical contents, defects and thus failure modes can be categorized as follows:

- Resource management,
- Check,
- Logic,
- Interface,
- Timing,
- Support,
- Larger defects, and
- Cosmetic.

**Resource management** failure is typically related to allocation, initialization, manipulation, consumption, and release of data, variables, or other resources.

A software system may fail if variables are uninitialized before use, since, for some languages such as C or C++, uninitialized variables may hold any value and the software behavior is non-deterministic. Variable values may also be assigned incorrectly, which is discussed under logic failures.

Faulty memory resource management exhibits as a memory leak after the system has been running for an extended time and allocated memory has not been properly deallocated after use. Quite often, a library function allocates a chunk of memory, populates it with necessary data, and returns it to the client code, but the client code does not free the memory after use. Code may deallocate memory twice (double free) through different paths; before the second free, the same memory may be allocated to other data. Code may also access the memory after deallocated (use after free), which can crash the system. When the system is low on memory and the code allocates an additional, perhaps, a large chunk of memory, but without checking whether the allocation succeeded or not, subsequent memory access (null pointer dereference) can crash the system. For allocated memory, it should be initialized or assigned first and then dereferenced.

Although code should not pass a pointer into data on the stack, programmers frequently commit the mistake without even realizing it. A trivial example is shown below:

```
char* getName() {
        char tmp[10];
        strcpy(tmp, "Mike Zhu");
        return tmp;
}
```

The memory for the char array tmp is allocated dynamically, and thus, it is stored in the stack. Once the function call getName() returns, no one knows what will be at the location tmp points into, particularly if there are other function calls before the pointer is actually used.

In many languages such as C-based ones, array is indexed from 0; in many other languages, array is indexed from 1. When a programmer switches among different languages, he may mistakenly write code where array index is off-by-one, which causes buffer overrun or overflow.

Access to resource can cause access violation failures. A user may have the privilege to access some system resources, but is improperly denied. A user who has no privilege to access some resources is granted the right. Or the code simply does not check whether the user has the privilege at all.

Precious system resources such as database connections, file handles, graphics device interface (GDI) handles on Windows, thread pool threads, and so on shall also be managed and recycled properly to guard against system instability.

**Check** failures are validation errors or incorrect responses when detecting an invalid value. For defensive programming, code shall assert or check variable values, function return values, and user inputs.

Quite often, code does not check null reference, and it can crash the program or throw an exception when the null reference is dereferenced. Some modern languages such as Java 8 and C# introduced "null-conditional operators" to avoid the issue, a binary operator which returns the second argument but null if the first argument is null. For example,

```
int? count = customers?[0]?.Orders?.Count();
```

The above C# code returns null, if customers is null, the first customer is null, or orders of the first customer is null. The code is certainly succinct and avoids the null reference exception, but does not solve the problem entirely.

Error handling code can be at fault as well. The code may miss an error handling, or the error recovery does a wrong thing. Although not an error, it is not a good idea to have an empty catch block. The code may return a status that does not match the program status; for example the code returns an OK code in the presence of failures (false negative) or an ERROR code when there is no failure involved (false positive). The client code may just ignore the status code returned. In object-oriented programming, exception class objects are raised and it is a common practice to handle specific exceptions before handling more generic ones. The code may mistakenly handle more generic exceptions first; thus, specific exceptions may never be handled.

**Logic** faults are related to comparison logic, control flow, computation, algorithms, and other logical errors.

Common failures related to comparison logic include incorrect use and compound of comparison statements. Code may use the negated conditions mistakenly. The operator precedence might be overlooked (&& is evaluated before ||). In compounded statements, parenthesis may be missing or misplaced, etc.

Simple typos alter code intention and cause problems without being detected for a long time, since it may have no syntactic errors. For example, we intend to compare a and b,

```
if (a==b) { ... }
```

but accidently write

```
if (a=b) { ... }
```

For C or C++, the statement a=b assigns b to a and returns the rvalue of the assignment, i.e., b. In the end, the value b is compared to 0 (false if b==0 and true otherwise).

As another example, we have a simple function, as coded here:

```
int getValue() {
    int value = 0;
    ...
    return value;
}
```

We intend to compare the function return value to another value, e.g.,

```
if (getValue()==bValue) { ... }
```

but commit a simple typo

```
if (getValue==bValue) { ... }
```

The code is syntactically fine. Instead of comparing the return value to bValue, the code compares the function pointer to bValue, which would be always false.

A non-trivial code unit typically has many branches, and which branches to execute are controlled by simple or compound conditional statements. In high-level programming languages such as C, C++, Java, or C#, if, if/else, switch/case, and loops (while, for, or do ... while) statements are used to decide the control flow.

In switch/case statements, a default case is often needed if there is no match with the cases, and the break statements are generally required to skip remaining cases including default. When the break statement is missing, the subsequent case(s) is executed (fall through), which changes the flow of execution.

In case of loops, the common faulty logic includes as follows: The loop is executed a wrong number of times including infinite loops, or each loop accesses wrong data in an aggregated data such as arrays. If the loop does not actively allocate memory, it may run forever and deprive the program to perform other tasks. The infinite loop may be triggered by a specific combination of input and thus may not be detected in testing. Similar to infinite loops, recursion without a base case will eventually exhaust the system resources (out of memory).

Each case in the switch/case or each condition in the if/else block is supposed to be independent. Common mistakes include overlapping logic and gaps in logic. Suppose a program checks the value of variable x and performs some action accordingly. The domain of x is the entire real number. A simple overlapping example is:

```
if (x < 5) {
    doSomething();
} else if (x > 3) {
    doSomethingElse();
}
```

The region (3, 5) is covered by both conditions. A simple gap in logic is:

```
if (x < 3) {
    doSomething();
} else if (x > 5) {
    doSomethingElse();
}
```

The region [3, 5] is covered by neither condition. While it is easy to spot the logic faults in the above examples, it is hard when multiple variables are involved.

Logic failures could also be caused by arithmetic operations. In scientific or engineering applications, software is used to perform the numerical calculation. Related to that, there might be overflow, underflow, and rounding issues. Additionally, the algorithm might not be valid for all input in the defined domain, or it might not have adequate accuracy. We call failure modes caused by the above reasons as a faulty algorithm. Examples of invalid math operations include divided by zero or non-positive input to a log function. Loss of arithmetic precision can happen in many different ways. Unlike math division, division of two integers often gives an integer as a quotient in programming. Underflow happens when a calculation result is smaller in magnitude than the smallest value the machine can represent—if that happens, using double instead of float might help. Overflow is just the opposite, and the calculation result is bigger than the type can represent. Loss of precision or overflow may also happen when a value or the result of a calculation is downcast to a different type, e.g., from double to float or from float to int.

Computation or round-off error can accumulate and become sizeable if not handled carefully. In computer graphics and animation, rotation matrix is used to manipulate objects. Over time as the errors accumulate, points that began as coplanar will no longer be coplanar, or a square starts to look like something other than a square due to shearing effects. To work around the potential issues, the rotation matrix can be built anew periodically.

To add up many numbers in an array or list, a straightforward way is to write a loop and add them one by one. However, when a few thousand numbers are added together, one loses the precision due to rounding errors, particularly when a small number is added to a big number. If the precision is important, we have a faulty algorithm here. When all numbers have a comparable magnitude, they can be added in a tree-like fashion, e.g., ((((item1 + item2) + (item3 + item4)) + ((item5 + item6) + (item7 + item7))) + ···). The Kahan summation algorithm also known as compensated summation is even more clever (https://en.wikipedia.org/wiki/Kahan_

summation_algorithm). It uses an extra variable to keep track and accumulate error, and when the error is large enough, it is accumulated to the sum.

We group faulty data in this category as well, which includes the failure modes like data does not match design in terms of intended use (scope, type, size, max/min/default, unit, purpose) and/or intended scope (global or class).

Incorrect assignment of a variable can cause failures. The incorrect assignment may be caused by failures in memory or just incorrect calculation. Failure in memory can be a result of unintended overwrites due to design errors, programming errors, or hardware failures. Incorrect calculation may be caused by faulty algorithms, improper scaling or measurement unit, stale data, overflow or underflow, etc.

**Interface** faults are errors when the code interacts with other modules, libraries, databases, file systems, operating systems, or hardware interfaces. As discussed in the previous chapter, we are not limited to API-like interfaces. Typical failure modes include incorrect interface call and correct interface call with incorrect parameters.

An interface function may be called in a wrong context. Syntactically, the interface call is correct, but not semantically. There is a precondition for an interface call, and the precondition may be violated. The postcondition for the interface call may be ignored or not checked.

An interface call is correct, but wrong parameters may be passed. The data may be stalled. The data may be in a different unit.

Faulty I/O is a special kind of faulty interface, and it can occur when a unit of code interfaces with a storage device or medium. There are two common I/O failure modes related to the file system and database objects. In the case of file, the code may open a non-existing file, write to a file that has not been opened yet or that was opened for read only, write incorrect data to a file, or write correct data to a wrong file. Most operating systems have a limited resource on file handles. If many files are open at the same time, it can cause problem. When multiple processes write data to the same file, the file access needs to be serialized. Operation on the database and database records has similar failure modes and root causes.

Remoting components or components hosted in different processes may communicate through interfaces. Due to overhead and latency in message exchanges, chatty interface is not recommended.

**Timing** failures are common in concurrent programming, where multiple execution units, threads, or processes use shared resources.

A race condition happens when two threads try to access (e.g., write) the shared data and the result depends on the order of the execution of the threads, which is not deterministic. To guard against the race condition, synchronization constructs such as monitor or semaphore can be used.

In multi-threaded programming, a deadlock can also happen. It is typically caused by inconsistent locking sequence in different threads. For example, thread A locks object a and is waiting for object b, while thread B locks object b and is waiting for object a. Neither thread can advance in this case. Deadlocks can be detected by using the lock graph to see whether there is a loop in it.

In general, it is not a good practice to check a condition of a shared variable, perhaps protected by a lock, inside a loop (spin lock) until it changes state. It just wastes clock cycles which can be used for other tasks. Instead, use proper synchronization constructs such as wait and notify.

A software module completes its tasks typically by interacting and cooperating with other modules. It may call other modules multiple times. A common failure mode, faulty sequence, is that the calling sequence is not right. It can also be the case that the preconditions for calling a function are not met. When repetition is required, the number of times to call can also be wrong.

**Support** defects are tangential to the code itself, but can nevertheless negatively impact code functionalities. Such issues may involve version control, build process, configuration of software, packaging, versioning, etc. In the case of version control, a wrong revision of code can be used in build, or code is accidently checked in and causes undesirable behavior. In the case of build process, the build is not from scratch when it is supposed to be; thus, an old version (e.g., object files) is used to build other DLLs or executables. It can also happen that a wrong library, sometimes incompatible, is linked during build process. When packaging the software, configuration files can be missing or incomplete, or wrong files are included; thus, the software is misconfigured.

**Large** defects involve more than one part of the module or code segment. A functionality is designed, but can be missing in code implementation. A design can also be partially implemented or implemented incorrectly. Fixing this type of issues typically requires large-scale modification to the current solution approach, thus large defects. Faulty functionality can happen if the code is not written to the design and requirements. Failure modes can be caused by missing code to implement functionalities assigned to the underlying code module, the code does not address the roles and responsibilities assigned to the module by the upstream design and requirements, or the code unit has extraneous code not related to any assigned functionality.

Large defects can also be traced to improper or incomplete design (faulty design functionality). Although we assume the requirements and upstream design are correct, we should log an obvious issue.

**Cosmetic** defects do not cause functional failure, but may cause other issues, for example, typos or incorrect messages displayed to users. They will not cause system failures, but are usually a good idea to correct.

In the above discussion, we did not discuss programming language or programming paradigm-specific issues and failure modes. For example, object-oriented programming can have its own specific failure modes and root causes such as virtual function overriding. One can supplement the above discussion as needed. We did not consider syntax errors, since they can be caught by compilers, and in modern practice, code is typically sent out for review after it has been compiled and sometimes unit tested. We did not single out errors related to test definition or execution either, since these errors can be classified into the discussed categories. Lastly, modern sophisticated static code analysis tools can be exploited to detect many issues discussed above probably except those in the support, large, and cosmetic categories, depending on the tool capability and desired level of false positives.

## 7.3   Code Evolvability Failure Modes and Root Causes

As software developers, a large part of our professional lives is spent on maintaining, adapting, correcting, perfecting, and modifying existing code. Empirical data show that developers spend about half of their time on reading and comprehending programs during software maintenance [39]. Thus, improving code evolvability is important to enhance developers' productivity. Code smells, however. Code smells are code structures that violate fundamental design principles and negatively impact design quality. We call those issues code evolvability defects.

Code with evolvability defects is not compliant with standards and is error-prone or difficult to understand, modify, and extend. About three-fourths of defects found during code review are related to software evolvability [41]. Addressing those issues will improve software evolvability by making the code easier to understand, modify, and extend. There are evidences that poorly structured software increases development effort and is correlated with lower productivity and more rework. Code layout and documentation as well as naming convention impact code comprehension, code test time, and debugging time. Evolvability defects have a clear economic importance [41]. Code smells or evolvability defects are usually not bugs, since they are not technically wrong and do not hamper current software functionalities. As they will slow down future development and increase the risk of serious software issues in later releases, they are considered technical debt, and it is a good idea to correct them to avoid future interest.

Evolvability defects are categorized as documentation, visual representation, and structure.

**Documentation** defects are related to commenting and naming of software elements that are part of the source code and communicate the intent of the code to readers. It is good to have a coding standard in place. This defect category further includes (a) language features and (b) textual. Modern programming language introduces some key words such as public/protected/private in Java or C#, which are used to document the code. Misuse of language features is considered a defect. Language feature misuse defects strongly depend on the programming language. Textual documentation defects include (1) uninformative names or names violating standards or conventions, and (2) missing comments or incorrect comments. Self-descriptive naming documents the code itself. Non-trivial programming logic warrants some explanation and rationalization.

**Visual representation** defects negatively impact program readability. It is typically caused by improper use of or missing white space such as indentations, space characters, and blank lines. Blank lines are often used to group logic code sections. It is also a good practice to break lengthy lines into multiple lines to avoid scrolling when reading the code.

**Program structure** is determined by the parser tree of the code and is not related to its visual representation or documentation, both of which will not change the parser tree. The type of program structure defects further includes solution approach and organization. While organization defects can be resolved by reorganizing the code, solution approach defects can be resolved by rethinking solution alternatives. Usually, detecting solution approach defects requires skills, experience, and context knowledge.

Many things can cause organization defects, and an organization defect can have different forms:

- A programming element may be misplaced in a wrong module/file or a wrong code section in the same module.
- A function is too long and has to be restructured.
- There is dead code that can never be reached, for any combination of input or for the permissible inputs the program is intended.
- Duplication of code or functionality can be removed. The DRY (do not repeat yourself) principle shall be followed.
- Complex code has to be simplified. Complex code is prone to errors and hard to test completely. KISS (keep it simple, stupid) is a well-regarded design principle. There are various metrics to measure the complexity of code.

Solution approach defects are more or less related to improper design instead of implementation. Examples may include:

- Change function. This can be as simple as to use a different function call. It can also include creating a new function, so it can be called in different places to avoid duplication of code.
- Use standard method, e.g., reuse an existing library instead of reinventing the wheel.
- Semantic dead code is the code that is executed at runtime, but serves no purpose. Although it does not do harm, it just wastes some clock time and memory space. Future code readers may be puzzled by its purpose.
- Semantic duplication is not syntactically duplicated, but with the same intent. An example may be two sorting implementations with similar running time complexity.
- Other miscellaneous, e.g., incorrect use of a data structure such as stack instead of vector.

Some of the structure defects could be detected in the design phase if design artifacts are reviewed. For example, programming elements need to be moved from one module to another module and the original location is specified in design. In general, defects in these categories are difficult for static code analysis tools to detect.

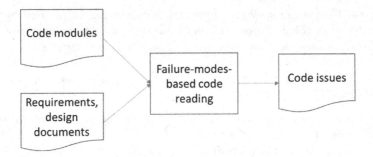

**Fig. 7.1**  Input and output for failure-modes-based code reading

## 7.4  Failure-Modes-Based Code Reading Techniques

With the discussion of functional and evolvability failure modes in the previous sections, we turn to the failure-modes-based code reading, which is schematically shown in Fig. 7.1.

The input to the failure-modes-based code reading includes code modules or source code files, along with the design documents. The requirements document may also be provided as input, and use cases can help readers understand how the software modules are used to fulfill system functions. Code modules are subject to review, but not the design or requirements documents. The output of code reading is a list of code issues, which can be sorted by their seriousness.

The failure-modes-based code reading instructions are listed in Fig. 7.2.

It is not possible to use the above reading instructions by a single code reader. We suggest the software team to divide the reading responsibility among multiple members with a different focus, e.g., documentation, code structure, solution approach, resources and interface, check, and logic. The idea behind the perspective-based reading can be utilized here to manage the complexity.

## 7.5  Example

Cross-correlation measures the similarity of two signals as a function of the displacement of one signal relative to the other. It has been utilized in many areas such as signal processing, image processing, and pattern recognition. Mathematically, cross-correlation is related to convolution of two signals; that is the convolution of f(x) and g(x) is the same as the cross-correlation of f(x) and g(−x), where f and g are two signals of variable x.

A. Understand the system requirements and design; select the most (safety and mission) critical and error-prone code modules for reading and analysis.

    a. If there are requirements and design for a critical part of the system, but no code modules can be linked to it, log an issue as missing implementation.

    b. For each of the selected code modules, understand their functionalities and design elements and verify the code implementation is complete, the code is not missing any aspects, and there is no extra code. If you fail to verify for any reasons, log an issue.

B. For each and every code modules identified,

    a. Use the list of common code failure modes and root causes defined by your organization, and verify that the failure modes and causes do not present in the code module. If you fail to verify, log an issue. In the end, go to step N below.

    b. If the list is not available, follow steps C-M below. If one particular step is not applicable or is not a concern, simply skip it.

C. Resource management failure modes

    a. Focus on primitive and composite data variables, particularly their allocation, initialization, manipulation, consumption, and release. Log an issue if

        i. Variables are uninitialized before use;

        ii. Allocated memory is not deallocated after use, particularly when memory is allocated and used in different places;

        iii. There is a (potential) double free through different paths, use after free, null pointer dereference;

        iv. A pointer into data on stack is passed around;

        v. Array lower and upper bounds are not checked or incorrectly checked (off-by-one).

    b. Focus on system resources usage. Log an issue if

        i. Access rights are improperly granted or denied, or the privilege is not checked;

        ii. Precious system resources, including database connections, file handles, GDI handles, thread pool threads, etc., are not managed (acquired/released, recycled).

**Fig. 7.2** Instructions for failure-modes-based code reading

D.  Check failure modes, focusing on data/user input, function returns. Log an issue if

    a.  Code does not check the null reference passed in or returned from a function call;

    b.  Code returns an incorrect status or error code; code does not check status or error code where it should;

    c.  There is no error handling or the error recovery is wrong;

    d.  In try-catch blocks, the caught exception types are not in the order of specific types first then general types.

E.  Logic failure modes, focusing on comparison logic, control flow, computation, algorithms, and other logical errors.

    a.  Log an issue on comparison logic failures if

        i.   Logic statements are incorrectly negated, operator precedence is not intended, or statements are incorrectly grouped;

        ii.  Logic comparison is written as assignment;

        iii. Function pointer is compared to values.

    b.  Log an issue on control flow failures if

        i.   There is a fall through failure in switch/case due to missing cases (including default) or break statements;

        ii.  A loop is executed incorrect number of times (including infinite loop), or data access is incorrect in each iteration;

        iii. A recursion has no base case to bottom out;

        iv.  There is an overlapping condition in if/else;

        v.   There is a gap on the domain of a variable covered by the conditions in if/else.

    c.  Log an issue on arithmetic operation failures if

        i.   There is a case of divide by zero of non-positive input to log function;

        ii.  There is overflow, underflow, including improper casting;

        iii. There is loss of precision due to single operation (e.g., int/int) or accumulated effects.

    d.  Log an issue on faulty data if

        i.   Data does not match design in terms of intended use (scope, type, size, max/min/default, unit, purpose) and scope (global or class);

        ii.  The operations on data are not correct (wrong

**Fig. 7.2**  (continued)

algorithm) or do not match its definition and purpose (e.g., improper scaling or wrong units).

F.  Interface failure modes. Focus on interfaces such as I/O, networking, database, etc. Log an issue if
   a.   Incorrect interface is called;
   b.   Interface is called with wrong parameters (staled data, data in wrong units, etc.);
   c.   Interface is called in a wrong context (precondition is not met);
   d.   Multiple interfaces are called in a wrong order;
   e.   A wrong or non-existing file is opened; read/write before the file is opened or opened for other modes; incorrect data is written to a file; data is read from file incorrectly.

G.  Timing failure modes in concurrent programming. Log an issue if
   a.   There is a potential race condition when more than one thread updating a shared variable with no synchronization;
   b.   There is a potential deadlock due to inconsistent locking;
   c.   There is a spinlock busy waiting.

H.  Support failure modes. Log an issue if
   a.   There is no version control or a wrongly versioned code is used;
   b.   The build is not from scratch when it is supposed to; a wrong library (wrong version or vendor) is linked;
   c.   Configuration files are missing, wrong, or incomplete.

I.  Large-scale failure modes. Log an issue if
   a.   Code is not written to requirements or designs;
   b.   Code is not addressing the roles and responsibilities assigned to it;
   c.   Code unit has extraneous code not related to any assigned functionality.

J.  Cosmetic failure modes. Log an issue if there are typos or incorrect messages displayed to users, or other situations of similar kind.

K.  Documentation failure modes. Log an issue if
   a.   Comments in code are missing, incorrect, or outdated;
   b.   Language features such as private/protected/public are not used properly;
   c.   Names of software elements do not follow standards or are not informative.

L.  Visual representation failure modes. Log an issue if whitespaces

**Fig. 7.2**  (continued)

(indentations, space characters, and blank lines) are missing or misused.

M. Program structure failure modes.
    a. Log an issue against code organization if
        i. A program element is misplaced;
       ii. A function is too long;
      iii. There is dead code or duplicate code;
      iv. Code logic is too complicated.
    b. Log an issue against solution approach if
        i. A different function call can be used, or a new function is needed;
       ii. A standard method is not used, but similar code is written;
      iii. There is semantic dead code (code executed with no impact to functionality);
      iv. There is semantic duplication (different codes with similar intent);
       v. Data structure is misused.
N. Sort the logged issues based on the severity of impacts and likelihood to happen, so that they can be prioritized and a targeted improvement can be implemented, including mitigation.

**Fig. 7.2** (continued)

In image processing, to take into account the intensity variation due to lighting and exposure conditions, zero-mean, normalized cross-correlation $\rho_{fg}$ is used, which is defined as

$$\rho_{fg} = \frac{1}{\sigma_f \sigma_g} \frac{1}{N} \sum_x [f(x) - \bar{f}][g(x) - \bar{g}],$$

where the barred signal indicates an average, $\sigma$ is a standard deviation, and N is the number of overlapping signals, pixels in this case. We shall understand x as a two- or three-dimensional (2- or 3-D) variable, but for the following discussion, x is treated as 1-D; that is the images are projected to form a 1-D signal.

Our purpose is to slide one signal against the other, compute cross-correlation at different displacements, and report the displacement where the cross-correlation is maximal. The C# code performing this task and subject to review is shown below:

```
01      public int FindMaxCorrPos(short[] f, short[] g) {
02          int fLen = f.Length, gLen = g.Length
03          int maxPos = 0;
04          double corr = 0, maxCorr = 0;
            // shift g (half length to the left & right) to match f
05          for (int x = -gLen/2; x < fLen-gLen/2; x++) {
06              int idx1 = Math.Max(0, x);
07              int idx2 = Math.Max(0, -x);
08              short fsum = 0, gsum = 0;
09              for (int i=Math.Max(0,x); i<Math.Min(fLen,gLen+x); i++) {
10                  fsum += f[idx1++];
11                  gsum += g[idx2++];
12              }
13              double invCounts=1/(Math.Min(fLen,gLen+x)-Math.Max(0,x));
14              double favg = fsum*invCounts;
15              double gavg = gsum*invCounts;

16              idx1 = Math.Max(0, x); idx2 = Math.Max(0, -x);
17              double ffsum = 0, ggsum = 0, fgsum = 0;
18              for (int i=Math.Max(0,x);
                       i<Math.Min(fLen,gLen+x); i++,idx1++,idx2++) {
19                  ffsum += (f[idx1]-favg)*(f[idx1]-favg);
20                  ggsum += (g[idx2]-gavg)*(g[idx2]-gavg);
21                  fgsum += (f[idx1]-favg)*(g[idx2]-gavg);
22              }
23              double fsigma =  Math.Sqrt(ffsum*invCounts);
24              double gsigma =  Math.Sqrt(ggsum*invCounts);
25              corr = invCounts*fgsum/(fsigma*gsigma);
26              if (corr > maxCorr) {
27                  maxCorr = corr;
28                  maxPos = x;
29              }
30          }
31          return maxPos;
32      }
```

Here is the high-level description of the code: Signal g is shifted and correlated to signal f, where one makes sure there is some minimal overlap of f and g (line 5). For each displacement x (for loop in line 5), the overlapping area is calculated (line 9), where i is used to index the location in signal f. Lines 9–12 calculate the average of two signals in overlapping region (barred f and g). Lines 18–25 calculate standard deviations and cross-correlation. Finally, lines 26–29 update the maximal cross-correlation and its displacement.

This short piece of code is not entirely made up, and in fact, some elements were taken from a student project. This code exhibits quite some issues:

- This is managed code and appears to have no apparent resource management issue. The array indices are carefully calculated (lines 6, 7, and 9), which is good.
- For the passed in arrays f and g, the code does not check whether the arrays are null or zero-length. If one of them is null, line 2 will fail; if one of them is

zero-length, line 13 will fail (divided by 0). There is no defensive checking nor exception handling.

• The code has a few logic issues.

a. The displacement with a maximum cross-correlation (maxPos) is set to 0 (line 3) as default, which is a valid value. If the loop at line 5 is skipped, this default maxPos is mistakenly returned.

b. At line 4, the maximum cross-correlation (maxCorr) is set to 0. The value of normalized cross-correlation is in the range of −1 and 1, inclusive. Therefore, 0 is an inappropriate value to start with.

c. At line 8, fsum and gsum are defined as short. Since they are used to accumulate the values in f and g, there is a risk of overflow.

d. Line 13 is meant to change a few divisions to multiplications to speed up the calculation. However, invCounts is 0, since int divided by int returns int. The denominator can also be zero as mentioned earlier.

e. When one signal is constant (in the overlapping region), then its standard deviation, as well as the cross-term fgsum (line 25), is zero. Therefore, corr will be NaN (not a number).

• The code is a truthful implementation of the definition of cross-correlation. However, looping the overlapping regions twice (loops at lines 9 and 18) is not necessary. With some simple arithmetic, one loop will be sufficient (in that case, one has to accumulate the sum of squared f and g), which is left for interested readers to experiment. Moreover, the array indexing is a bit slow in managed code. Once code errors are debugged out, one can consider using unsafe code to improve the speed performance. Furthermore, as mentioned earlier, cross-correlation and convolution are related and fast Fourier transform can be used to speed up the convolution. The brute-force calculation of convolution or cross-correlation is $O(N^2)$, where N is the length of the signal sequence. With fast Fourier transform, the calculation can be reduced to $O(N \log N)$, which is a significant speedup when N is large.

## 7.6   Summary

All software systems have to be implemented using one or more programming languages. Program code often has errors, which can be classified as functionality and evolvability defects. This chapter surveyed common functional defects that include resource management, check, logic, interface, timing, support, larger defects, and cosmetic and evolvability defects that include documentation, visual representation, and structure. Based on those common failures and causes, we devised code reading techniques, which guide readers in their code review process to improve their defect detection capacity.

# Chapter 8
# Failure-Modes-Based Usability Reading

Software can fail due to poor usability, and focusing on usability is the easiest and cheapest way to improve user's perceived system quality. This chapter discusses the software usability failure modes and common causes and presents a failure-modes-based reading technique to detect and remove the software usability deficiency.

## 8.1 Usability and Usability Evaluation

Usability is concerned how easy it is for a user to perform a desired task and what supports a system provides to the user to accomplish the task. It comprises the following aspects: learning system features, using the system efficiently, minimizing the impact of errors, adapting the system to user needs, and increasing the user's confidence and satisfaction [4]. System designers and human factors engineers work together to optimize human performance by designing systems to match cognitive and physical capabilities and limitations of human users. For many desktop, Web, and mobile applications, usability is the final arbiter of quality. Experiences indicate that focusing on usability is the easiest and cheapest way to improve the user's perceived system quality.

Usability problems can be detected with usability testing or usability analysis [63]. Usability testing is also known as user-based usability evaluation. In usability testing, usability problems are found through the observation of and interaction with users while they use or comment on a user interface. Usability analysis is also known as usability inspection. In usability analysis, problems are found through the expertise of analysts and analytical techniques they employ. Heuristic evaluation, cognitive walk-through, and guidelines and checklists are common analytical techniques in practice. One may find many informative heuristics on Wikipedia (https://en.wikipedia.org/wiki/Heuristic_evaluation). Usability analysis costs much less than usability testing.

© The Author(s) 2017
Y.-M. Zhu, *Failure-Modes-Based Software Reading*, SpringerBriefs in Computer Science, https://doi.org/10.1007/978-3-319-65103-3_8

FMEA is another analytical approach, which allows analysts to understand the user-related risks associated with a device or software by focusing on end users and how they could use, misuse, and even abuse the product. To that end, a full-fledged use FMEA can be conducted, which typically involves a team in multiple meetings. Alternatively, a software FMEA can take a usability viewpoint as Neufelder suggested [42]. Here, we employ the usability viewpoint, analyze the common software failure modes and root causes related to use and misuse, and use those to guide analysts' individual reading and analyzing activities.

## 8.2    Usability Failure Modes and Root Causes

A good user interface design should make it easy to do the right thing and hard to do the wrong thing. Despite all good attention, failures still occur. A system failure can happen due to human error using the software or human misuse of the software [42]. A formal usability has an aspect of the efficient use of the software. Since we are concerned here with the safety and risks related to the product, we concentrate our discussion on potential failures and pay attention to the possibility of the user using the product incorrectly, either risking the integrity of the product or creating an unsafe situation.

Human errors can be caused by cumbersome operations software provides, particularly when there is no readily available guidance on actions and workflow. When there is a mismatch between the user's mental model and the user interface or workflow design, the user may find the software awkward or difficult to use. The user may have acquired the mental model from other similar applications, industry standards, domain models, or reference architecture.

Inconsistencies among software itself can also cause human errors. An inconsistency can be as simple as the inconsistent use of terms in different sections of the user interface or in different screens. The inconsistency might be caused by the fact that the same design principles were not carried out consistently throughout the system, or that the system was evolved during a long period of time, and many people and teams across the globe contributed, who perhaps never met each other during the product lifetime.

When many tedious steps are required to accomplish a task, particularly if those steps are arranged in a seemly illogic manner, the user's mental load is high and it is hard to focus and not to make a mistake. Even on a single user interface, if the interface contains too much information (text, instructions, widget controls, etc.), the display looks busy and cluttered and the user is hard to get oriented. For text, make sure the color and font size are appropriate.

Human errors can be caused by the lack of robustness in software for common errors. Ideally, the software shall make it hard for a human to make mistakes. For data entry, the user will appreciate the hints on the expected data format and default values. As another example, if the user is deleting an important file or piece of data, the software shall ask the user to confirm the action in case the user accidentally triggered that action or simply the user changes mind; if the user is closing the program, but did not save the modified data yet, the software shall give the user an opportunity to save the data before quitting the program. Undo and redo operations shall be provided as part of the standard operations. However, do not overdo it. It is really annoying if the user needs to confirm every single operation or if there are many pointless message boxes which the user has to dismiss one after another.

If the operation of the software makes a faulty assumption on how and when the software will be used in the field, which is not met in the deployment, the software may fail to perform as well. One frequent faulty assumption is that human will attend the software system all the time. The reality is that the user may be multi-tasking, thus not focusing on the software all the time. The other frequent faulty assumption is that the user will notice the alert or alarm right away and has enough time to consult online help files and address or correct the errors. However, the user may not see the alert; even if he or she saw the alert, he or she may not have access to the online help; and even if he or she gets hold of the online help, he or she may not locate the relevant contents right away.

User documentation can also be at fault. There may not have the operator's manual; or the document is hard to read, understand, and act upon; or the document itself is not correct or outdated. All these situations will lead to user mistakes.

The user may unintentionally misuse the software. For example, the user may use the software for an unsupported feature or perform the tasks or actions not appropriate or allowed by their roles. The user can be accidentally granted permission to read or write data or execute commands. Conversely, the user can be accidentally deprived the right to read or write data or execute commands.

From an error handling perspective, the user has a problem with adverse effects and needs to correct the problem. Thus, the usability goal is to minimize the chance to commit an error (error prevention), help the user understand the situation with appropriate information once errors happen, allow the user correct errors or recover from errors (error recovery), and deal with system failure appropriately.

## 8.3  Failure-Modes-Based Usability Reading Techniques

With the above information on usability failure modes and failure causes, we are ready to discuss the failure-modes-based usability reading techniques.

As shown in Fig. 8.1, input to failure-modes-based usability reading is mainly the user interface design or screen captures, with supporting user's manual, help files, etc. All the input is subject to review for usability gaps. The output of failure-modes-based usability reading is a list of usability issues or concerns.

The detailed instructions for failure-modes-based usability reading are shown in Fig. 8.2.

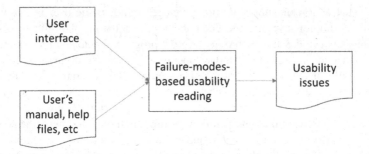

**Fig. 8.1** Input and output for failure-modes-based usability reading

## 8.4   Example

For the purpose of this example, let us assume you are reviewing a GUI element that allows the users to calculate body mass index (BMI), given weight and height. That simple utility can be a part of a Web page or embedded in other applications. You may find the background information in Sect. 6.4 is useful. The screen capture is shown below:

Body Mass Index (BMI)

Weight (lb):

Height (ft):

BMI:                          Calculate

This is a simple UI, with only a few controls. A user can enter weight in pounds and height in feet, then click on Calculate to have the BMI calculated and displayed. We notice the following issues, however:

- It is fine to use the US customary units instead of the metric systems. Height, however, oftentimes is represented as, e.g., 5 feet and 11 inches. It is cumbersome to request the user to convert 5 feet and 11 inches into 5.92 feet. It is even worse if the height is entered as 5.11. Therefore, it works better to provide two fields, for feet and inches, respectively.
- It is not necessary for the user to click on "Calculate" to get back BMI. Instead, once the weight and height are filled in, the BMI can be calculated automatically without user's request.

A.  Identify user actions and associated user interface screens that are most critical and risky.
B.  For each action/screen
   a.  Identify failure modes and root causes for human errors, and their effects.
      i.   Identify any cumbersome operations without action or workflow guidance. Focus on mismatches between mental models vs interface or workflow design. Log any issues found.
      ii.  Identify any inconsistency among software itself, including usage of terms, labeling, style, design, colors, etc. Log any issues found.
      iii. Identify any tedious operation steps related to a task, busy or cluttered screens with text, instruction, widgets, etc. Log any instances found.
      iv.  Check the robustness of the software on common user errors. For example, there shall be a confirmation message if a user is about to delete a file or piece of data, a prompt message to save the data when the user is quitting the application, undo and redo operations related to complex tasks. Log issue if there is lack of robustness.
      v.   Identify any faulty assumption on how and when the software is used; for example, does it require operator's attention all the time? Does it require operator's intervention right away? Log as issue if the assumption will not meet in reality.
   b.  Identify failure modes and root causes for misuses, and their effects. Log an issue if
      i.   The software allows the user to perform an unsupported feature,
      ii.  The software allows the user to perform an action which should not be allowed for his role, or
      iii. The software does not allow the user to perform an action which should be allowed for his role.
   c.  Identify failure modes and root causes for error handling, and their effects. Log an issue if the software
      i.   Does not prevent the user from committing an error,
      ii.  Does not provide any information to allow the user

**Fig. 8.2** Instructions for failure-modes-based usability reading

                understand the situation once an error occurs, or

        iii.  Does not allow the user to correct errors and recover from errors.

C.  Log an issue if there is no operator's manual, the document is hard to read, understand, and act upon or not localized, or the document is incorrect or outdated.

D.  For logged issues, sort them based on the severity of impacts and likelihood to happen so that they are prioritized for a targeted improvement.

**Fig. 8.2**  (continued)

- From this UI, it is not clear whether both weight and height textboxes prevent the users from entering non-numerical values. This simple rule can be easily enforced.
- The display of BMI value is treated the same as the values of weight and height, which can be changed by the users. The BMI value should not be user changeable.
- The utility of this simple UI can be improved if additional information is provided, e.g., if the BMI value falls into the normal or overweight range, with appropriate color coding.
- BMI values for adults or children are used and interpreted differently. They also vary with sex, population, and other factors. A similar, yet simple note shall be provided to avoid misuse or misinterpretation.

## 8.5  Summary

Improving system usability is the easiest and cheapest way to improve the user's experience with your system. Due to poor usability design, a user may misuse or abuse system features, which can cause harm. We surveyed the common failure modes and their root causes in the area of usability. Based on the survey, we designed failure-modes-based usability reading techniques. A good user interface design shall also optimize the user interactions with the system and improve (expert) the user efficiency and productivity, which was not covered since we focused on failure modes here. Readers thus shall use the failure-modes-based usability reading as a supplement to other usability inspection methods.

# Chapter 9
# Failure-Modes-Based Test Reading

When a responsible organization or analyst team conducted a software FMEA, it is reasonable to assume that all single failure modes have been addressed and failure modes with high risk have all been identified. This chapter discusses how the software FMEA outcome can be used to direct software testing and verify that failure modes causing serious consequences have been eliminated or compensated for.

## 9.1 Introduction

As a part of software FMEA, the preventive measures, corrective actions, and compensating provisions are often identified for failure modes and root causes to mitigate their effects [42]. The correctness and effectiveness of these mitigations need to be verified in the finished product, however. In this chapter, we discuss how a tester can utilize the software FMEA outcome and test the correctness and effectiveness of the preventive measures, corrective actions, and compensating provisions, which focuses the tester on most critical and risky areas. The tester may need to simulate the underneath faulty conditions with fault injection technique, also known as fault insertion testing (FIT), to conduct some tests. Software FMEA and FIT are complementary to each other, and together, they enhance each other's value. The reading technique discussed in this chapter is different from the failure-modes-based reading techniques presented in the proceeding chapters, which detect and remove failure modes in software artifacts (requirements, design, code, and user interface).

Software FMEA can be used as a list of potential test cases [47]. It also provides information on fault insertion points and parameters to execute FIT. Failure modes are converted into test cases by writing procedures to simulate conditions that lead to the failure. Test cases are created for failure modes/root causes without prevention and detection methods. To utilize the test resources optimally, more testing efforts can be directed to failure modes/root causes with high RPN values.

© The Author(s) 2017
Y.-M. Zhu, *Failure-Modes-Based Software Reading*, SpringerBriefs
in Computer Science, https://doi.org/10.1007/978-3-319-65103-3_9

## 9.2   FMEA and Testing

Software testing is much more than we can treat in this chapter. Tons of books have been written on it. We highlight a few best practices here, however. Tests shall be performed in a real environment. When testing against requirements, make sure we test both shall and shall-not requirements. To grow software reliability, test cases shall reflect the operational profile. Stress testing is indicative of how the system will behave in extreme situations. If your system uses legacy code, commercial-off-the-shelf (COTS), or software of unknown provenance (SOUP) software, make sure that industry-specific practices are followed, anomaly lists from software suppliers are reviewed, and the code is tested for your usage scenarios. Testing shall focus on what matters to users and on critical and risky areas. This chapter provides help in testing of critical and risky areas.

As discussed in Chap. 2, after failure modes and root causes have been identified, the consequences of those failure modes are analyzed. Effects on components, subsystem, system, and sometimes humans are captured. Any known preventive measures are documented as well. The severity of the effects and the likelihood that could happen are assessed, and the RPN is calculated. The mitigation phase of the FMEA follows the above analysis. When identifying mitigation, potential corrective actions and compensating provisions are identified, and the RPN is revised if needed.

Software FMEA also identifies process controls that are employed during software development life cycle. Those process controls include following design or coding standard to avoid fault injection; performing design review, code review, and other analysis to detect and remove defects; and executing software reliability growth testing. Those process controls are not discussed since they are not related to execution-based software testing.

A preventive measure is a mechanism in place to prevent the associated failure modes from happening [42]. To cope with the failure mode due to a low data transfer rate, one could increase the network bandwidth; to deal with a memory leak, more memory can be put into the system. The effectiveness of a preventive measure has to be tested and confirmed.

A corrective action could be to change software requirements, design, code, or user interface, so that failure root causes are entirely removed [42]. Usually, a corrective action like this eliminates failure modes completely. When the failure causes cannot be eliminated entirely, the occurrence of the failure cause can be reduced by, e.g., architectural fault management tactics. There is no specific testing required except to verify that the software artifacts are updated.

Corrective actions also include documented or well-known workarounds. A workaround is a different way to complete a functionality, performed by the end users. It is not considered a preventive measure. N version programming is often practiced to improve software reliability through built-in fault tolerance or redundancy, where multiple copies of similar implementation from the same specification are employed and a voting scheme is adopted to pick one answer from multiple available results. Workarounds are not N version programming. To invoke a workaround, a user typically changes the workflow or the way he or she interacts with the software explicitly, while the N independent versions of the implementation are executed at the same time and the end users may not be aware of their presence. The effectiveness of workaround shall be not only documented, but also verified for correctness and effectiveness.

Despite all efforts to eliminate root causes thus failure modes, in the end, certain failure modes will stay. Some failure modes can be mitigated by updating the user's manual, providing help files, enhancing user training, or improving the user interface design (e.g., raise audible and visible alerts when a potential failure mode occurs). If we cannot prevent and eliminate a failure, we could employ a monitoring tactic to mitigate risk. With an independent software component, the health of other components or the whole system can be monitored. Any abnormal behavior is corrected dynamically at runtime (e.g., restarting a component) or brought to the user's attention for his or her intervention. All those changes shall be verified for effectiveness.

During FMEA, many failure modes might have been considered. Corrective actions can also be doing due diligence and adding test cases to ensure that specific failure modes will not happen. This makes sense particularly if the failure effects can be caught in routine testing or testing with minimal additional efforts.

Lastly, compensating provision is an option to mitigate failure risk [42]. Typically, a compensating provision is not performed with the same software. When memory leak prevents the system from functioning properly, rebooting the system and restarting the software application is a compensating provision. When a system continues to operate in the presence of failure, human intervention can be a compensating provision. At one time, this author sent a postscript file to a printer, but the printer continued to print out garbage. Intervention early by stopping the printing saved a tree or two.

Failure modes and root causes may not have a preventive measure, corrective action, or compensating provision, particularly when the RPN is deemed acceptable. It is our recommendation that the test plan shall consider them. Test designers need to think hard and come up with creative test cases to ensure that the severity and the likelihood of occurrence are reasonable and the risk is indeed acceptable.

## 9.3  FMEA-Based Test Reading Techniques

With the above discussion of the preventive measures, corrective actions, and compensating provisions, we are ready to discuss FMEA-based test reading. The main idea of FMEA-based test reading is to reference the FMEA spreadsheet and make sure that the preventive measures, corrective actions, and compensating provisions associated with failure modes and root causes are verified for correctness and effectiveness in the finished product. FMEA-based test reading is not meant to replace any existing test reading a software organization may have in place; rather it is complementary to existing test reading techniques. An existing test reading technique may trace and ensure that every requirement is tested, which is not the objective of FMEA-based test reading.

FMEA-based test reading is schematically illustrated in Fig. 9.1. The input of FMEA-based test reading includes a software FMEA spreadsheet and a test plan, and the output of the reading is a list of observations. Only the test plan is subject to review for defect detection, however. We are not dictating a specific format or template of the FMEA spreadsheet. But at minimal, the software FMEA spreadsheet shall have columns on failure modes, root causes, effects, preventive measures, severities, occurrences, initial RPNs, corrective actions, compensating provisions, revised RPNs, etc., and an example is shown in Fig. 9.2. The test plan shall have a detailed list of test cases. In addition to listing test cases for all software requirements, the test plan shall have test cases to verify the preventive measures, corrective actions, and compensating provisions associated with software failure modes and root causes. An observation shall be made if any such test case is missing, deemed incomplete or ineffective, or for whatever reason, the reader considers the test case defective.

A software organization may have established guidelines on well-formed test cases. For example, each test case shall be (a) traceable to a requirement; (b) clear on setup, execution steps, expected behaviors, and input and output data;

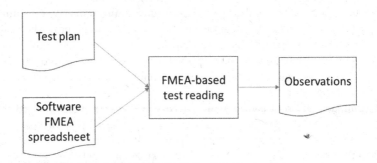

**Fig. 9.1** Input and output of FMEA-based test reading

**Fig. 9.2** A typical spreadsheet to support software FMEA

| ID | Component | Failure Modes | Root Causes | Local Effects | System Effects | Preventive Measures | Severities | Occurrences | Initial RPNs | Corrective Actions | Compensating Provisions | Revised RPNs |
|----|-----------|---------------|-------------|---------------|----------------|---------------------|------------|-------------|--------------|--------------------|--------------------------|--------------|
|    |           |               |             |               |                |                     |            |             |              |                    |                          |              |

A.  Using the initial RPN values, pick the most risky "failure mode and
    root cause" entry among the remaining entries in the software FMEA
    spreadsheet and do the following:

    a.  If there is a preventive measure captured for this failure
        mode and root cause,

        i.   Search the test plan to locate a test case that verifies
            the preventive measure. If no test case is found, log
            an observation against the test plan.

        ii.  Read the test case for correctness, completeness, and
            effectiveness. If the test case is incomplete,
            ineffective, or simply defective, log an observation
            against the test plan.

        iii. If multiple preventive measures were captured,
            repeat the above two steps (i) and (ii) for each
            remaining measure.

    b.  If there is a corrective action captured for this failure mode
        and root cause,

        i.   If the corrective action eliminates the failure mode
            and its root cause entirely, skip remaining steps for
            this corrective action and go directly to step (iv)
            below. However, it is desirable to design a test case,
            e.g., stress testing or repeated testing, to verify that
            the root cause for the failure mode is indeed eliminated.

        ii.  Search the test plan to locate a test case that verifies
            the corrective action. If no test case is found, log an
            observation against the test plan.

        iii. Read the test case for correctness, completeness, and
            effectiveness. If the test case is incomplete,
            ineffective, or simply defective, log an observation
            against the test plan.

            1.  If the corrective action is a documented
                workaround, make sure the test case includes
                steps to check the existence of the document
                and to evaluate the correctness of the
                document. Additionally, the workaround
                itself shall also be tested.

            2.  If the corrective action involves the user's
                manual, help files, user training, or the user
                interface design, make sure the test case has

**Fig. 9.3** Instructions for FMEA-based test reading

elements to check the existence, correctness, and effectiveness of the corrective action.

3. If the corrective action is to monitor health of the component or system, make sure the test case has the relevant steps to monitor and correct the abnormal behaviors, and the test itself is sound.

4. If the corrective action is to have a test case to ensure that the root cause and failure mode will not occur, evaluate if the test case is adequate for its purpose.

iv. If multiple corrective actions were captured, repeat the above steps (i)-(iii) for each remaining actions.

c. If there is a compensating provision captured for this failure mode and root cause,

i. Search the test plan to locate a test case that verifies the compensating provision. If no test case is found, log an observation against the test plan.

ii. Read the test case for correctness, completeness, and effectiveness. If the test case is incomplete, ineffective, or simply defective, log an observation against the test plan.

iii. If multiple compensating provisions were captured, repeat the above steps (i) and (ii) for each remaining provisions.

d. If there is no preventive measure, corrective action, or compensating provision captured for the failure mode and root cause, make sure there is a test case to ensure that the severity and the likelihood are reasonable and the risk is indeed acceptable. If there is no test case on that regard, log an observation against the test plan.

B. Repeat until all "failure mode and root cause" entries have been exhausted or the allocated time runs out.

**Fig. 9.3**  (continued)

(c) understandable and runnable by testers and with an unambiguous oracle; (d) adequate for its purpose; and (e) free of typos and grammatical errors. Although important, the well-formedness applicable to general test cases is not the focus of FMEA-based test reading.

Detailed steps of FMEA-based test reading techniques are listed in Fig. 9.3. As steps A and B indicate, this reading technique is risk-driven. Step B has two options: The reading can take whatever time it needs to finish all failure modes and root causes, or the reading can be time-boxed. In either case, the most risky areas are examined first. If there is not enough time, the most risky areas are guaranteed to be examined. Most risky areas deserve more test cases to cover different aspects. The other steps in Fig. 9.3 regarding the preventive measures, corrective actions, and compensating provisions are self-explanatory.

## 9.4 Example

In automated retinal image processing, it is important to locate and segment the optic nerve head (ONH), e.g., when assessing the progression of glaucoma. State-of-the-art segmentation algorithms cannot guarantee to locate and segment optic disks with 100% accuracy in terms of location and size, particularly on diseased eyes.

Suppose a software FMEA has been conducted on the segmentation algorithm and the final results agreed by the analysis team are captured in the following table. Here, the template in Fig. 9.2 is used, except the roles of rows and columns are switched for proper display. There may be other failure modes and root causes, but due to space limitation, we only focus on two here.

| ID | 100 | 101 |
|---|---|---|
| Component | Segmentation | Segmentation |
| Failure modes | No ONH segmented | Incorrect ONH segmentation |
| Root causes | Incorrect ONH location | Correct ONH location, but incorrect shape |
| Local effects | No ONH identified | ONH incorrectly identified |
| System effects | No image analysis results | Incorrect image analysis results, misinformation for diagnosis |
| Preventive measures | N/A | N/A |
| Severities | 5 out of 10 | 8 out of 10 |
| Occurrences | 2 out of 10 | 2 out of 10 |
| Initial RPNs | 10 | 16 |
| Corrective actions | (a) Alert users that the ONH could not be localized (b) Document the limitation in the user's manual (c) Provide a manual tool to allow the users to locate the ONH | (a) Compare the sizes to standard width and height; if the difference is more than 2 times of standard deviation, alert the users (b) Document to remind the users verifying the results visually (c) Provide a manual tool to allow the users to define manually |
| Compensating provisions | N/A | N/A |
| Revised RPNs | 3 (S3 × L1) | 8 (S8 × L1) |

We here discuss how a tester can reuse the software FMEA results. It is not feasible to list all test cases here. Rather we discuss, based on the software FMEA results, what test cases shall be considered.

- The likelihood of occurrence for both root causes is rated as 2 out of 10. This shall be checked in the predefined population of retinal images, including diseased and healthy retinas.
- Three corrective actions are listed for the root cause "incorrect ONH location." With those corrective actions, both severity (to lose a key system function) and occurrence likelihood are reduced.

    (a) If a particular retinal image used for testing cannot trigger the cause, a fault shall be inserted to test whether users are alerted upon failure.
    (b) It shall be verified that the user's operation manual reminds the users this potential algorithm limitation.
    (c) A manual workaround is provided as a corrective action. It shall be verified that the workaround is documented in the user's manual and the workaround itself is tested.

- Three corrective actions are listed for the root cause of incorrect ONH shape at a right location. While the corrective actions do not change the severity (incorrect results and misinformation for diagnosis), the likelihood of occurrence is reduced.

    (a) ONH is a vertical oval, with a typical size of 1.76 mm horizontally and 1.92 mm vertically. Faults shall be inserted to verify that when the segmented ONH size is strongly deviated from the standard, the users are alerted.
    (b) It shall be verified that the user's operation manual includes a passage that reminds the users to check the segmentation results.
    (c) A manual workaround is provided as a corrective action. The users shall be able to modify and edit the segmented ONH. This is different from the other workaround where the user places the location of ONH.

## 9.5  Summary

A responsible organization shall create a complete software FMEA that captures all single failure modes and root causes and identifies most critical failure modes and their consequences on local and system effects. Most risky failure modes and root causes shall be dealt with during system development, prevented entirely, detected and mitigated, or compensated for. The effectiveness and completeness of the preventive measures, corrective actions, and compensating provisions shall be verified, along with assumptions adopted during analysis. This chapter presented a FMEA-based test reading, structured to meet the above objective.

# Chapter 10
# Conclusion

Software programs have bugs, and it is costly to fix them, particularly when they are found late in the development phases or even worse when they are detected after the software is released. Software peer review is the proven, effective, efficient, and operable method to detect and remove defects early. To reduce variability and improve individual's performance in detecting defects, software review is often augmented with software reading techniques which guide readers where and how to look for problems. Software review has been applied in almost all kinds of software projects. However, it often detects only style and trivial defects.

Software failure mode and effect analysis was introduced about the same time as software review was. It allows system designers to think through potential problems and figure out how to detect, prevent, or mitigate them before they materialize and create a catastrophe; i.e., it prevents problem and enables engineers to design quality and reliability into a system. Software FMEA is good to exhaustively categorize faults and their effects at both low and high levels. However, it is widely recognized and documented that software FMEA is tedious, error-prone, and time-consuming to execute. As a result, it has been applied only to safety and mission critical systems.

To take the benefits of software FMEA to more software practitioners while avoiding the tediousness of software FMEA and to enable software reviews to detect critical rather than trivial or style defects, this book espoused the essence of software review and software FMEA and developed a failure-modes-based software reading approach. Based on the analysis of common failure modes, root causes, and mitigation, specific reading techniques were created for software requirements specifications, design, coding, usability, and test plans. Failure modes guide readers what to look for, root causes provide cues where to look, mitigations prompt readers to check whether any features are missing or inadequate, and reading techniques prescribe steps to conduct reading and detect defects.

The developed failure-modes-based software reading techniques are risk-driven and intended to find critical defects with lower cost (compared to software FMEA) which are often missed with other reading techniques. The reading techniques are

© The Author(s) 2017
Y.-M. Zhu, *Failure-Modes-Based Software Reading*, SpringerBriefs
in Computer Science, https://doi.org/10.1007/978-3-319-65103-3_10

useful and beneficial to software practitioners in their individual preparation for software reviews or software FMEA, particularly for those in small teams or resource-constrained organizations.

We shall point out that the family of reading techniques focuses on detecting critical defects, and thus, it shall be used as complementary to other reading techniques in order to detect and fix all kinds of defects. The list of failure modes and root causes used in reading must be tailored to the systems at hand and is expandable to include the experience and expertise of your organizations or teams. We tried to provide a relatively comprehensive list, which shall be customized to team needs. The literature has a vast collection of software quality assurance methods, each with its own strength and weakness. We expect that software peer review with the failure-modes-based reading techniques is used in a complementary manner, along with other tools and methods.

# About the Author

**Yang-Ming Zhu** is a software architect at Philips HealthTech and has 18-year industry experience in software engineering. He is the author of "Software Reading Techniques" (Apress, 2016) and practices software FMEA on medical devices. His research and development interest focuses on software engineering and image processing, as well as applications of machine learning in these areas. He is a senior member of IEEE, holds the Software Architecture Professional Certificate from the Software Engineering Institute at Carnegie Mellon University, and has Ph.D. in physics, MS in computer science and in biomedical engineering, and BS in biomedical engineering. He authored or coauthored 80 chapters and scientific journal papers, and invented or coinvented 9 issued US patents.

© The Author(s) 2017
Y.-M. Zhu, *Failure-Modes-Based Software Reading*, SpringerBriefs
in Computer Science, https://doi.org/10.1007/978-3-319-65103-3

# References

1. Banerjee, N.: Utilization of FMEA concept in software lifecycle management. In: Proceedings of Conference on Software Quality Management, pp. 219–230 (1995)
2. Basili, V.,. Caldiera, G., Lanubile, F., Shull, F.: Studies on reading techniques. In: Proceedings of the Twenty-First Annual Software Engineering Workshop, SEL-96-002, pp. 59–65 (1996)
3. Basili, V.R., Sekby, R.W.: Comparing the effectiveness of software testing strategies. IEEE Trans. Softw. Eng. **13**(12), 1278–1296 (1987)
4. Bass, L., Clements, P., Kazman, R.: Software Architecture in Practice, 3rd edn. Addison-Wesley (2013)
5. Becker, J.C., Flick, G.: A practical approach to failure mode, effects and criticality analysis (FMECA) for computing systems. In: Proceedings of IEEE High-Assurance Systems Engineering Workshop, pp. 228–236 (1996)
6. Bidokhti, N.: FMEA is not enough. In: Reliability and Maintainability Symposium, pp. 333–337 (2009)
7. Bosu, A., Carver, J.C., Bird, C., Orbeck, J., Chockley, C.: Process aspects and social dynamics of contemporary code review: insights from open source development and industrial practice at Microsoft. IEEE Trans. Softw. Eng. **43**(1), 56–75 (2017)
8. Bowles, J.B., Wan, C.: Software failure modes and effects analysis for a small embedded control system. In: Proceedings of Reliability and Maintainability Symposium, pp. 1–6 (2001)
9. Broy, M., Kirstan, S., Kremar, H., Schatz, B., Zimmermann, J.: What is the benefit of a model-based design of embedded software systems in the car industry? In: Emerging Technologies for the Evolution and Maintenance of Software Models, Chap. 13 (2012)
10. Brykczynski, B.: A survey of software inspection checklists. Softw. Eng. Notes **24**(1), 82–89 (1999)
11. Chen, Y., Ye, C., Li, G.: Failure mode databases and their knowledge-based management. In: International Conference on Reliability, Maintainability and Safety, pp. 732–736 (2014)
12. Chillarege, R., Bhandari, I.S., Chaar, J.K., Halliday, M.J., Moebus, D.S., Ray, B.K., Wong, W.Y.: Orthogonal defect classification—a concept for in-process measurement. IEEE Trans. Softw. Eng. **18**(11), 943–956 (1992)
13. Ciolkowski, M., Laitenberger, O., Biffl, S.: Software reviews: the state of the practice. IEEE Softw. **20**(6), 46–51 (2003)
14. Committee on the Safety of Nuclear Installations: Failure Modes Taxonomy for Reliability Assessment of Digital Instrumentation and Control Systems for Probabilistic Risk Analysis, NEA/CSNI/R(2014)16 (2015)
15. D'Ambros, M., Bacchelli, A., Lanza, M.: On the impact of design flaws on software defects. In: Proceedings of the 10th International Conference on Quality Software, pp. 23–31 (2010)
16. Denney, E., Trac, S.: A software safety certification tool for automatically generated guidance, navigation and control code. In: IEEE Aerospace Conference (2008)

© The Author(s) 2017

Y.-M. Zhu, *Failure-Modes-Based Software Reading*, SpringerBriefs in Computer Science, https://doi.org/10.1007/978-3-319-65103-3

17. El-Haik, B.S., Shaout, A.: Software Design for Six-Sigma: A Roadmap for Excellence, Chap. 16. Wiley (2010)

18. Fagan, M.E.: Design and code inspections to reduce errors in program development. IBM Syst. J. **15**(3), 182–211 (1976)

19. Failure Mode/Mechanism Distribution—FMD-2016, Reliability Information Analysis Center (2016)

20. Firesmith, D.: Security use cases. J. Object Technol. **2**(3), 53–64 (2003)

21. Firesmith, D.: A taxonomy of testing. https://insights.sei.cmu.edu/sei_blog/2015/08/a-taxonomy-of-testing.html. Accessed 10 Apr 2017

22. Fragola, J.R., Spahn, J.F.: The software error effects analysis: a qualitative design tool. In: Proceedings of IEEE Symposium on Computer Software Reliability, pp. 90–93 (1973)

23. Gamma, E., Helm, R., Johnson, R., Velissides, J.: Design Patterns: Elements of Reusable Object-Oriented Software. Addison-Wesley (1994)

24. GJB/Z 299C-2006: Reliability Prediction Handbook for Electronic Equipment (2006)

25. Goddard, P.L.: Software FMEA techniques. In: Proceedings of Annual Reliability and Maintainability Symposium, pp. 118–123 (2000)

26. Hatton, L.: Testing the value of checklists in code inspections. IEEE Softw. **25**(4), 82–88 (2008)

27. Huang, B., Zhang, H., Lu, M.: Software FMEA approach based on failure modes database. In: 8th International Conference on Reliability, Maintainability and Safety, pp. 749–753 (2009)

28. IEC 60812: Analysis Techniques for System Reliability—Procedure for Failure Mode and Effects Analysis (FMEA), 2nd edn. (2006)

29. IEEE Std 1028-2008: IEEE Standard for Software Reviews and Audits (2008)

30. IEEE Std 1044-2009: IEEE Standard Classification for Software Anomalies (2009)

31. Johnson, P.M., Tjahjono, D.: Does every inspection really need a meeting? Empir. Softw. Eng. **3**, 9–35 (1998)

32. Kessentini, M., Kessentini, W., Sahraoui, H., Boukadoum, M., Ouni, A.: Design defects detection and correction by example. In: 19th IEEE International Conference on Program Comprehension, pp. 81–90 (2011)

33. Leveson, N.: Safeware: System Safety and Computers. Addison-Wesley (1995)

34. Lutz, R.R.: Analyzing software requirements errors in safety-critical, embedded systems. In: IEEE International Symposium on Requirements Engineering, pp. 126–133 (1993)

35. Lutz, R.R.: Targeting safety-related errors during software requirements analysis. J. Syst. Softw. **34**(3), 223–230 (1996)

36. Lutz, R., Nikora, A.: Failure assessment. In: 1st International Forum on Integrated System Health Engineering and Management in Aerospace (2005)

37. Lutz, R.R., Woodhouse, R.M.: Contributions of SFMEA to requirements analysis. In: Proceedings of the 2nd International Conference on Requirements Engineering, pp. 44–51 (1996)

38. Lutz, R.R., Woodhouse, R.R.: Requirements analysis using forward and backward search. Ann. Softw. Eng. **3**, 459–475 (1997)

39. Maalej, W., Tiarks, R., Roehm, T., Koschke, R.: On the comprehension of program comprehension. ACM Trans. Softw. Eng. Methodol. **23**(4), Article 31 (2014)

40. Mannion, M., Keepence, B.: SMART requirements. Softw. Eng. Notes **20**(2), 42–47 (1995)

41. Mantyla, M.V., Lassenius, C.: What types of defects are really discovered in code reviews? IEEE Trans. Softw. Eng. **35**(3), 430–448 (2009)

42. Neufelder, A.M.: Effective Application of Software Failure Modes Effects Analysis. Quanterion Solutions (2014)

43. Ozarin, N.: The role of software failure modes and effects analysis for interfaces in safety- and mission-critical systems. In: IEEE Systems Conference (2008)

44. Ozarin, N.: Applying software failure modes and effects analysis to interfaces. In: IEEE Reliability and Maintainability Symposium, pp. 533–538 (2009)

45. Ozarin, N., Siracusa, M.: A process for failure modes and effects analysis of computer software. In: Proceedings of Annual Reliability and Maintainability Symposium, pp. 365–370 (2003)
46. Parnas, D.L., Weiss, D.M.: Active design reviews: principles and practices. In: 8th International conference on Software Engineering, pp. 215–222 (1985)
47. Pentti, H., Atte, H.: Failure mode and effects analysis of software-based automation systems. STUK-YTO-TR 190 (2002)
48. Porter, A.A., Votta, L.G.: An experiment to assess different defect detection methods for software requirements inspections. In: Proceedings of the 16th International Conference on Software Engineering, pp. 103–112 (1994)
49. Porter, A.A., Votta, L.G., Basili, V.R.: Comparing detection methods for software requirements inspection: a replicated experiment. IEEE Trans. Softw. Eng. 21(6), 563–575 (1995)
50. Price, C., Snooke, N.: An automated software FMEA. In: Proceedings of the International System Safety Regional Conference, Singapore (2008)
51. Reifer, D.J.: Software failure modes and effects analysis. IEEE Trans. Reliab. 28(3), 247–249 (1979)
52. Research Information Letter 1002, Identification and analysis of failure modes in digital instrumentation and controls (DI&C) safety systems—Expert clinical findings, part 2, US Nuclear Regulatory Commission (2014)
53. Rigby, P.C., Bird, C.: Convergent contemporary software peer review practices. In: Proceedings of the Joint Meetings of the European Software Engineering Conference and the ACM SIGSOFT Symposium on the Foundations of Software Engineering, pp. 202–212 (2013)
54. Ristord, L., Esmenjaud, C.: FMEA performed on the SPINLIE 3 operational system software as part of the Tihange 1 NIS refurbishment safety case. CNRA/CSNI Workshop on Licensing and Operating Experience on Computer-based I&C Systems, vol. 2, pp. 37–50 (2001)
55. Schneidewind, N.F., Hoffmann, H.M.: An experiment in software error data collection and analysis. IEEE Trans. Softw. Eng. 5(3), 276–286 (1979)
56. Shull, F.: Software reading techniques. In: Encyclopedia of Software Engineering. John Wiley and Sons (2002)
57. Tian, J.: Software Quality Engineering: Testing, Quality Assurance, and Quantifiable Improvement. Wiley-IEEE Computer Society (2005)
58. Vaandrager, F.: Does it pay off? Model-based verification and validation of embedded systems. PROGRESS Whitepaper, 2006. http://www.ita.cs.ru.nl/publications/papers/fvaan/whitepaper/whitepaper.pdf. Accessed 10 Apr 2017
59. Votta Jr., L.G.: Does every inspection need a meeting? In: Proceedings of the ACM SIGSOFT Symposium on Foundations of Software Engineering, pp. 107–114 (1993)
60. Walia, G.S., Carver, J.C.: A systematic literature review to identify and classify software requirement errors. Inf. Softw. Technol. 51, 1087–1109 (2009)
61. Wallace, D.R., Kuhn, D.R.: Failure modes in medical device software: an analysis of 15 years of recall data. In: IEEE International Conference on Computer Systems and Applications, pp. 301–311 (2001)
62. Wang, W., Zhang, H.: FMEA for UML-based software. World Congress on Software Engineering, pp. 456–460 (2009)
63. Zhang, Z., Basili, V., Shneiderman, B.: Perspective-based usability inspection: an empirical validation of efficiency. Empir. Softw. Eng. 4, 43–69 (1999)
64. Zhu, Y.M.: Software Reading Techniques. Apress (2016)

Printed in the United States
By Bookmasters